BLACK ECONOMICS

Solutions for Economic

and Community Empowerment

by

Jawanza Kunjufu

AFRICAN AMERICAN IMAGES

1991

Chicago, Illinois

Cover illustration by Napoleon Wilkerson

Photo credits: William Hall

First edition, first printing

Copyright 1991 by Jawanza Kunjufu

BLACK ECONOMICS

Solutions for Economic and

Community Empowerment

DEDICATION REQUEST

Please pass a copy of this book

to someone unemployed

or someone who wants

to start their own business.

Table of Contents

Introduction

I have always wanted to write a book on economic development.

All my degrees are in economics, marketing and business. I became a published writer in 1978 with, *"Children Are The Reward of Life,"* and eight other books followed: *"Countering The Conspiracy To Destroy Black Boys, Volume I,"* in 1982; *"Developing Positive Self-Images and Discipline in Black Children,"* in 1984, *"Motivating and Preparing Black Youth to Work"* and *"Countering The Conspiracy To Destroy Black Boys, Volume II,"* in 1986, *"Lessons From History: A Celebration In Blackness,"* both Elementary and High School Editions in 1987, *"To Be Popular or Smart: The Black Peer Group,"* in 1988, *"Critical Issues In Educating African American Youth,"* in 1989, and *"Countering The Conspiracy To Destroy Black Boys, Volume III"* in 1990.

All of my previous books have addressed the issues of education, Black culture, and self-esteem. And yet all my degrees are in business. I noticed, when I was in college, that the people who had the financial resources very seldom had the social agenda, and those who had the social agenda very seldom had the economic resources. I decided then what I needed to do was to major in business and minor (or take additional courses) in Black studies. When I first became a writer and a public speaker, my desire was to exclusively do that and immerse myself in research, travel around the world (especially to Africa), and study more about our ancient civilization. I began to notice that there are an awful lot of people in the African American community who have degrees and a wealth of skills, but they seldom use these skills to employ people in their community.

I often ask people in my listening audience how many people do they employ. I also remind the audience that in the African American community the largest employers have become the military, McDonald's, and drug dealers. It is the responsibility of us all to do whatever we possibly can to employ ourselves, spouses, children, neighbors, and people in the larger community.

When I first became a speaker, I believed in my talents so much that I volunteered to do workshops for free. I simply asked the coordinator if I could be allowed to provide a book display. In those early years, the book sales financed the operation. I can look at each book that I've written or now published and I can tell you which employee was added on to our staff with that particular publication. I am very proud that the books have created a multi-million dollar communications company that is involved in publishing and distributing books, providing consulting services, creating a multi-cultural curriculum, SETCLAE, and a full feature movie, "Up Against the Wall." One major reason this book has been delayed is because I wanted to wait until my company had proven that Black-owned businesses can succeed.

Another major reason why it has taken so long to write *Black Economics* is because I've noticed at conferences, when the participants have to choose between a workshop on African history, male-female relationships, politics, education, or economic development, invariably the workshop on economic development will be the least attended. Ironically, in the other workshops there will be some discussion about the need to develop an economic base so that our researchers can develop historical documents and the need to create economic stability so that husbands and wives can remain together. There will be a brief discussion on which comes first economics or politics. They often choose politics and then spend the remaining time agonizing over an inadequate campaign budget. The participants in the educational workshop will propose the need for after school cultural programs, opening full-time schools, and then will discuss fundraising strategies.

In order to enhance Black economic development, we need families, churches, community organizations, and the media to accent and reinforce Black business owners so that we can increase the number of men and women who will consider this as much of a viable option as working for Fortune 500 companies. The Majestic Eagles, a group committed to stimulating Black business development, is doing an excellent job encouraging entrepreneurship. In my home town Chicago, there is a fruit stand owned by foreigners in our community that brings in over $2 million a year. There are many African American professionals who would not want to own a grocery store. They believe it is more prestigious to work downtown, than to work in a community and manage a fruit stand where they only see sales of $5 and $10 per customer, but at the end of the year the total sales are over $2 million. I've had that same kind of experience being the owner of a publishing company. I've seen professionals look at me and wonder why would someone stand behind the book table and sell $4.95 books when he possesses a Ph.D.? It would seem so much more financially viable to work for a large corporation. I've enjoyed watching a $4.95 book employ approximately 100 people and produce a full feature movie. I have yet to see a worker in corporate America do likewise.

There are several objectives that I would like to achieve in this book and they are as follows:

(1) We need to increase Black businesses in the African American community. For every 1000 members there are nine businesses, while in the larger White community there are 64 businesses per 1000.[1]

(2) We need to have our best African American minds involved in starting these businesses. Research has shown that in the African American community people who start businesses primarily have the least education and less capital and are primarily involved in the retail industry.

(3) We need to improve the environment for Black business development and stimulate and encourage participation. Presently, we have too many parents telling their children to get a good education to secure a "good job." There is also the image that Black businesses are marginal and as a result the illusion is that it's better to be a professional than to be a entrepreneur.

(4) We need Black institutions i.e., churches and civil rights organizations to begin emphasizing economic development and place it higher on the agenda. For some reason, we are the only ethnic or racial group who has developed a political base before an economic base.

(5) We need to stop waiting for governmental assistance and reparations to eradicate the implorable conditions that presently exist in the African American community.

(6) We need responsible business owners who will be responsive to the needs of the masses. We do not need the Black elite to encourage the masses to "Buy Black" for their aggrandizement, nor do we need owners who have no responsibility to give back to the masses that supported the business endeavor.

(7) Lastly, we need to study successful economic ventures historically and presently in our community. We have seen too much research, painting a victim analysis. At this juncture in our history, we need more case

studies of how families and companies, in spite of racism and monopoly capitalism, became successful.

I accept the fact that the majority of our community will be consumers not business owners, therefore, we need a more committed and educated Black consumer base that will be loyal to Black businesses, committed to saving money, and more astute to marketing practices that affect consumer expenditures.

There are many people addressing the economic issues affecting the African American community, some are actively involved in running multi-million dollar businesses. They are featured in *Black Enterprise* magazine. Others are actively involved with the government and affirmative action. There are members of the nationalist community that are advocating a separate land base and cooperative economics. There are conservatives who feel that the government should do less and that the burden and responsibility should be placed on the individual.

American economists define full employment somewhere between four and seven percent. This is designed so that capitalists will always have a labor reserve to draw upon so that wages can be kept at a lower scale and they will always have access to additional workers. From the African perspective, our goal should not be how wealthy any one of us can become, but what we can do for the benefit of 35 to 40 million Africans in this country, ultimately 900 million to a billion around the world.

Black Economics is divided into eight chapters. The first chapter is The Present Status, followed by The History of Black Economic Development, Why Foreigners Do So Well, The Global Economy, Obstacles To Black Economic Development, Responsibility Of Being an African American Consumer, Starting Your Own Business, and Black Economic Empowerment. My initial desire with this book was to increase the number of African American businesses. Previously, I mentioned the ratio is only nine per 1000, while the national average is 64 per 1000. Fundamentally, I feel that Africans were brought to America to work. We have worked the plantations and the factories, but with high technology and the exportation of jobs there is now less need for our labor. It becomes imperative that African Americans need themselves by creating jobs in their own communities. Unfortunately, I accept the reality that the majority of our people are not going to start their own businesses; even if we reach the national average, 936 people out of a thousand will not be involved in business formation. They too have a role to play just as White, Asian, and other consumers play a very fundamental role in the maintenance of their businesses. This book is not only designed to increase Black business formation, it is also designed to make the Black consumer more economically literate and supportive of the overall health of the African American community.

To God be the Glory and to Whom Much is Given, Much is Required!

Chapter 1

The Present Status

In the powerful book by Sydney Wilhelm *Who Needs The Negro*, he raises the question, "Why were negroes brought to this country?" Of course, the obvious answer is that we were brought to this country to work. Then he raises the next question, "Does that reason exist today?" If you look at the African American community and the unemployment problems nationwide, the answer to the second question is a resounding NO! And then he raises the last question, "What do you do with a people that you no longer need?" I often ask my audiences, when was the last time that the African American community was at full employment. The answer is 1865. That was the last time all African American people were working. Present statistics in the African American community concerning unemployment are from 25 to 30 percent for the adult community and 50 to 70 percent for African American teenagers, depending upon whose conducting the survey. I believe it's the larger figure.

> People in and out of the African American community ponder why so many African American men are on the corner in the middle of the day.[1]

In 1910, 90 percent of African American children had their fathers at home. In 1960, the figure dropped slightly to 80 percent, and in 1990, the figure had declined to 38 percent. Those three time periods represent what Alvin Toffler refers to as the three waves in the American economy. The first wave was agriculture, the second, industrialism, and the third is post industrialism, automation and the computer.

"Let me give some examples of how the new technology, which is more capital than labor intensive, has played a major impact on lower skilled people. Cleveland Electric Illuminating Company Conventional Plants employ 100 men to turn out 290,000 kilowatt hours of electricity. It's a new plant incorporating many new automatic devices and requires only 28 men to produce 420,000 kilowatt hours. This is over one-third more electricity than put out by the conventional plant using about one fourth the man power. Ford Bank installed an automated electronic accounting system. It employed 400 people. After installation, the same accounting department retained 75 workers whose output is twice that of the original staff. The Raytheon Manufacturing Company replaced its radio assembly plant with automatic equipment. This reduced its work force from 200 to two people. By the installation of computers, the United States Veteran's Administration released all but 300 of its 17,000 employees who previously processed insurance claims.

> It is estimated that if the computers presently in use by the federal government were discarded and the task performed by the computers was still required, a 100,000 additional individuals would have to be added to the payroll. The combination of mechanical and automatic processes allows the Ford Motor Company to turn out a block of a car in less than 15 minutes. This process previously required nine hours. In 1910, 104 men produced a single car. Now it only takes six men working less hours to accomplish the same feat.[2]

It used to be that an African American male in Detroit could drop out of high school in his junior year and work in one of the big three automobile plants and earn between 10 and 15 dollars an hour, and because of a strong union, receive adequate medical benefits, vacation, and a lucrative retirement package. The above scenario no longer exists for teenagers, still dropping out in great numbers in many cities, to earn that kind of money. The reality is that African Americans still have the same desires and needs that they had in the 1930s, 40s, and 50s in the 1990s, but the new economy is no longer paying $18 an hour for a low skilled position. Those jobs either have been eliminated, shipped over seas, or have been phased out due to the utilization of robots.

The impact of the automobile plants leaving many midwestern cities, the impact of Armour Meat Packing Company abandoning East St. Louis, Campbell Foods deserting Camden, NJ, U.S. Steel vacating Gary and Pittsburgh, and Agribusiness leaving places like Tupelo, MS have made these towns and so many others look like ghost towns. Many people feel that the African American community resembles more a colony than it does a community within the richest country in the world. Let's briefly describe the characteristics of a colony in the chart below and see if it portrays the demographics of the African American community.

Characteristics of a Colony
1) Low Per Capita Income
2) High Birth Rate
3) High Infant Mortality Rate
4) A Small/Weak Middle Class
5) Low Rate of Capital Formation and Domestic Savings
6) An Economy Dependent on External Markets
7) Major Export is Labor
8) A Tremendous Demand for Products Consumed by Wealthier Nations
9) Most of the Land and Businesses Are Owned by Foreigners
10) Indigenous Entrepreneurship is Limited[3]

I mentioned East St. Louis, Camden, Gary, and Tupelo in particular because when we move into the last chapter, Black Economic Empowerment, my recommendation is that those four cities with such large African American populations are four significant areas. These moderate size towns, if we are serious about economic empowerment, make excellent initial projects. It has been said that in the African American community that the three largest employers are the military, drug dealer, and McDonald's. The only argument is which one is the largest employer because all three are fighting for the number one position. There are estimates that one-third of the military is made up of African Americans. There are projections in large cities like Washington, D.C. and New York that one of every four African American males is either a drug user or a drug dealer. The only other option if they choose not to go to the military or deal drugs is to work at McDonald's for minimum wage. These are very limited options that presently exist in the African American community.

There has been a popular debate in the African American community about the two options of selling drugs and working at McDonald's. Many adults feel that the suggestion of McDonald's should not be made into a mockery. It is a legal source of income teaching work skills that can be transferable to other companies. The myth also needs to be put to rest that the option is either selling drugs at a $1,000 a week or making a $100 a week working at McDonald's.

The reality from a study done by the Rand Corporation in 1988 indicated that the average drug dealer was making approximately $700 a month. There were studies done at San Francisco State University, a Rockefeller study, and a narcotic and drug team research reflected that probably less than 20 percent of the people engaged in drug dealing have a net cash return of a $1,000 a month. Less than five percent of all people who deal drugs have a cash income that allows them to purchase expensive cars.

> The big profits in the drug trade do not come until one reaches a mid-level sale position. This includes the "beeper boys" so called because of their reliance on beepers and cellular phones. They have built up enough of a regular clientele to retire from direct street selling. Customers call them directly to make appointments for buys. In any case, most street level dealers can not hold on to profits from dealing because they are drug users themselves.[4]

The relationship of the African American community to the larger White community not only resembles a colony but the historical gap in income levels between the Black and White community has not narrowed in the past 20 years. Listed on the following pages are tables of median family incomes between 1970 and 1989 with a comparison of the median family income for Blacks to Whites, the percentage, the Black/White gap, and the total gap in dollars.

What is significant about this table (#1) is that there actually has been a decline in progress between 1970 and 1989. In 1970, the median African American family earned 61 percent of White family income. In 1989, this percentage had declined to 56 percent. In addition to that, there has been a consistent pattern between 1970 and 1989, averaging around 57 percent. This is consistent with America's perception of African Americans being three-fifths of a person or 60 percent. This is in stark contrast to the conservative administration that gives the illusion that there has been progress made in race relations and in income and that whatever other disparities exist are a result of a lack of initiative and self-reliance rather than institutional racism.

> The issue of civil rights had been a major public concern in the mid 1960s, but it has been declining in popularity for the past 25 years. Surveys show that Whites believe that the problems have been solved. Almost three-fourths of Whites surveyed in 1989 believed that opportunities had improved for Blacks during the Reagan Era.[6]

(Table #1)

Median Family Income

	Black	White	B/W	B/WGap	Aggregate Gap
1989	20,209	35,975	0.562	15,766	$127 Billion
1988	20,260	35,549	0.570	15,289	116 Billion
1987	20,091	35,350	0.568	15,259	116 Billion
1986	19,917	34,857	0.571	14,940	109 Billion
1985	19,344	33,595	0.576	14,251	104 Billion
1982	17,473	31,614	0.553	14,141	95 Billion
1980	19,073	32,692	0.583	13,619	87 Billion
1978	20,690	34,933	0.592	14,243	84 Billion
1970	20,067	32,713	0.613	12,646	64 Billion

Source: U.S. Bureau of the Census, Money Income and Poverty Status in the U.S.: 1989s

The assumptions that the remaining problems stem from deficient minority aspiration, culture, and family structure dominate the federal executive branch. Micro solutions of self-help to macro problems have given great prominence to conservative researchers Thomas Sowell, Charles Murray, Glen Loury, and Shelby Steele.

What makes the economic analysis more complex is the widening gap between the Black have's and the Black have nots. Listed is a table (#2) describing the percentage of Black families receiving income in various categories.

It is erroneous to stereotype the African American community and make it monolithic when 33 percent of African Americans live below the poverty line and 25 percent makes over $40,000. A book could be written on the various reasons for this gap and what can be done to close it. This gap was originally created with the division of house Negroes by the ruling class who recognized a need to have a buffer class large enough to convince the masses that whatever bleak conditions they were experiencing was due to their lack of initiative and ability. During the Civil Rights era of the 1950s and 60s and the Black Power Movement of the 1960s and 70s, the middle class was able to negotiate for additional crumbs from the table but unfortunately did not negotiate and demand equity for the entire race.

> Over 50 percent of college educated African Americans derive their income from the government, while less than two percent of all African Americans secure their income through business ownership. Thirty-five percent secured from private enterprise and less than five percent secured their income through business ownership.[8]

In this chapter on the present status of the African American community, we have to also look at our level of wealth as it relates to the larger White community. Table (#3) describes the median wealth of Blacks and Whites and where the various assets are distributed.

As a result of the first table where we earn 57 percent of Whites, and a White male who possesses a high school diploma earns more than a Black male with a college degree, our income is short by $127 billion. This also affects wealth where the shortage is $695 billion. These are the kinds of monies that the African American community needs to have if it's going to grow and develop. You can not have a shortfall in income of a $127 billion and in wealth of $695 billion and expect growth. If you also look at the table you will also see the disparity in most categories line by line with the largest percentage of equity in a motor vehicle.

In the African American community estimated income is $280 billion to $300 billion. This places the African American community as the ninth wealthiest nation/colony in the world. Unfortunately, there is a tremendous balance of payment problem in the African American community because 93 percent of our income is spent outside of the community. Listed below are the total receipts earned by African American businesses.

The total was a little over 21 billion dollars and is broken down by various categories and compared to the total receipts of all companies in America. Many African American businesses are marginal, 89 percent don't employ anyone, and their average annual receipts are $11,400. Only the top three percent have sales greater than one million dollars, and employ in excess of five workers.[11]

In addition to that, following are some of the leading categories of Black owned firms:
1) Business Services - 59,167
2) Health Services - 30,026
3) Special Trade Contractors - 29,631
4) Trucking & Warehouse - 19,663
5) Real Estate - 15,552
6) Amusement/Recreation Services - 13,250
7) Social Services - 13,210
8) Eating/Drinking Places - 11,834
9) Auto Repair/Garage Services - 11,801 [12]

Timothy Bates has provided an excellent analysis in his latest book *The Role of Black Enterprise in Urban Economic Development*, indicating that the largest number of new businesses are started by African Americans with less education and primarily in traditional lines of businesses, retailing, and personal services. This group has the highest failure rate. In contrast, a smaller number of African American entrepreneurs who have a greater level of education and are entering emerging areas that are skilled intensive services and wholesale.

In a later chapter, The Global Economy, an analysis is provided comparing the minuscule level of Black businesses as seen in this table to the larger White community. The comparison between the Black Enterprise 100 and the Fortune 500 reflects the naivete of anyone who thinks the stimulation of Black business develop-

(Table #2)

	1989		1988		1978		1970	
	Black	White	Black	White	Black	White	Black	White
Under $5,000	11.2	2.6	11.9	3.0	8.1	2.4	8.4	2.3
Less Than $10,000	25.9	7.7	27.3	8.5	25.4	8.5	24.6	8.0
$10,000-$34,999	46.5	40.7	46.7	43.2	51.2	47.7	56.3	45.4
$35,000-$50,000	27.5	51.6	25.9	48.4	23.3	43.8	19.2	46.6
More Than $50,000	13.8	30.9	12.6	27.4	10.0	21.1	6.7	23.2

Note: Totals will not equal 100.00 due to overlap of categories.
Source: U.S. Department of Commerce, Bureau of the Census, Money Income and Poverty Status in the U.S.: 1989s

(Table #3)

	Black Mean	White Mean	Black%	White%	B/W	Black Aggregate*	White Aggregate*	Aggregate* Gap*
Net Worth	$24,168	$103,081	100.00	100.00	23.45	$299,813	$7,766,444	$695,808
Interest Earning at Financial Institutions	3,743	20,137	43.80	75.40	10.80	15,590	1,143,952	128,787
Regular Checking	715	1,131	32.00	56.90	35.56	2,176	48,474	3,942
Stock & Mutual Funds	3,359	33,067	5.40	22.00	2.49	1,725	548,099	67,451
Equity in Business	40,593	77,008	4.00	14.00	15.06	15,440	812,278	87,077
Equity in Motor Vehicle	4,115	6,814	65.00	85.50	44.34	25,431	454,362	31,913
Equity in Home	35,718	62,016	43.80	67.30	37.47	148,762	3,144,555	248,111
Equity in Rental Property	45,542	88,155	6.60	10.10	33.75	28,582	670,827	56,083
Other Real Estate	17,221	41,901	3.30	10.90	12.43	5,404	344,198	38,037
U.S. Savings Bond	657	3,133	7.40	16.10	9.63	462	38,005	4,334
IRA or Keogh	4,109	10,802	5.10	21.40	9.06	1,992	174,168	19,989

Source: U.S. Department of Commerce, Bureau of the Census, Household Wealth and Asset Ownership: 1984

	Black Receipts	Total Receipts	B/T**	Receipt Gap	Black Firms	Total Firms	B/T**	Firm Gap
Total	21.6	$10,828	0.016	$1,299	424	17,526	0.198	1,713
Construction	2.5	561	0.037	66	37	560	0.539	32
Manufacturing	1.1	2,899	0.003	353	8	642	0.102	70
Transportation and Public Utilities	1.7	827	0.017	99	37	735	0.412	53
Wholesale Trade	1.4	1,335	0.009	161	6	641	0.070	73
Retail Trade	6.4	1,641	0.032	194	66	2,658	0.204	258
Finance, Insurance, and Real Estate	0.9	1,652	0.004	201	27	1,426	0.155	147
Selected Services	6.7	907	0.060	104	210	7,095	0.242	656
Other Industries*	0.9	1,006	0.007	122	34	3,769	0.075	425

Note: 1987 dollars were converted to 1989 dollars using CPI-U.

*Includes Agriculture, Mining, and Industries not elsewhere classified.
**This is Black receipts or firms per capita divided by the complement for total per capita. Black population in 1987: 29,417,000: total population in 1987: 241,187,000.
*(10)Source: U.S. Department of Commerce, Bureau of the Census, Survey of Minority - Owned Businesses: Black, 1987, and The Statistical Abstract of the United States, 1990, Table 859, p 521.

ment solely can employ the African American community.

In the final chapter on Economic Empowerment, we will look at this point because I am concerned with the critics of Black business development who conclude their speeches and books with a request from the master in the public and private sector.

One of the easiest ways to take a glance at Black business development is to look at the advertisers in *Essence* and *Ebony* Magazines. Its obvious that White companies are very much aware of the potential $300 billion spent and it also shows the dismal state of Black business development. In one of the latest issues of *Essence*, there were 48 full page ads and only two of them were from African American companies. They were both hair care companies. There were 17 cosmetic ads, four car ads, two cigarette ads, 19 miscellaneous ads, and one liquor ad. The inside front cover was for cosmetics, the inside back cover was for food, and the outside back cover was for liquor. In one of the current issues of *Ebony*, there were 76 full page ads and only one was an African American company, excluding publisher John H. Johnson, who advertises in his magazine. There were 31 miscellaneous ads, 11 liquor ads, 18 car ads, eight food ads, two cosmetic ads, and two cigarette ads. The inside back cover was a car. The inside front and back covers were for cigarettes. This is an unofficial qualitative look at the state of Black advertising and the interest in the ninth richest market in the world.

I'm pleased to see a much greater interest in conducting Black expos nationwide. Historically, what was designed to be a showcase for Black entrepreneurs became a greater representation of the Fortune 500. It becomes imperative that coordinators, if the objective is to feature African American establishments, don't use the Expo as an opportunity to make money by charging higher prices that only the Fortune 500 can afford.

> A major issue that needs to be addressed is land. In 1910, we owned 20 million acres and six million in 1970. We presently own less than four million acres. Currently, we are losing 500,000 acres of land per year.[13]

This figure would have been lower without the tremendous help of the Southern Cooperative and Land Association that is trying its best to provide legal assistance and technical training for family members and farmers that want to maintain their land.

It was a tragedy to hear about Hilton Head, S.C., where African people have owned land since slavery, but real estate developers have come in and converted the area into luxury estates and vacation paradise. Taxes have increased to the extent that many African Americans in the area are unable to pay them and literally are coerced into selling their property. African Americans love the area so much, they moved into smaller towns in the nearby area and are bused into Hilton Head to work on what are now called "Luxury Plantations."

Large numbers of African Americans believe that freedom will come from politicians. There is an erroneous belief that African American mayors can turn around Philadelphia, Detroit, Gary, Chicago, New York, Baltimore, Washington, and so many others. In an excellent book titled *The Closing Door*, by Gary Orfield and Carole Ashkinaze, the impact of African American mayors on Atlanta is analyzed. There is an image that Atlanta is a very progressive city, with a Black mayor, for the past two decades. It is a city with a large educational community containing a large number of Black colleges. It was the home of Dr. Martin Luther King, the civil rights movement, and the slogan, 'Atlanta is too busy to hate.' The authors illustrate that the same income disparity between Blacks and Whites for the entire country parallels itself in Atlanta. Atlanta's housing patterns were based on race and were as segregated as Chicago's.

> The Black middle class left the inner city and moved to the southern suburbs, while the White middle class and new jobs moved to the northern suburbs. Poverty actually increased during the Jackson\Young administration, while simultaneously 21 Black millionaires were created by the tremendous leadership of Maynard Jackson to create set-asides for the building of the Atlanta airport.[14]

The above analysis reinforces my contention and others' that to employ the masses of our people requires more than the election of politicians, especially at the local level, where there is less economic influence. In my home town, Chicago, there were African Americans who believed that with the election of Harold Washington, the projects would come tumbling down and that every one would secure a job. African Americans felt so strongly about this that voting records were documented with an

83 percent voter turnout. What African Americans found out in reality was that it did not matter whether it was Byrne, Bilandic, Washington, Sawyer, or Daley, there would still be projects, unemployment, and a marginal Black middle class. The unfortunate result is that African Americans, upon the death of Harold Washington, allowed their voting percentage to decline to 40 percent.

At the state and national levels, we have a smaller percentage. There is a greater degree of power both economically and politically since The Reagan and Bush administration created an environment of conservatism which brought on the Crosen versus Richmond decision and a critical look at minority set-asides. Under the past leadership of Congressman Parren Mitchell, pressure had been placed on the federal government to create legislation passed in 1986 mandating that five percent of the Department of Defense procurements be set-aside for minority owned businesses and historically Black colleges. This legislation in and of itself created 387 billion dollars worth of procurement opportunities. Fourteen other additional federal agencies including the Department of Energy, Interior, Transportation, and NASA also agreed to participate in this minority set-aside program.

The Supreme Court ruled in favor of Crosen; that the city of Richmond had discriminated against him because of the minority set-aside program. Many cities such as Atlanta, Richmond and others had developed very successful minority setaside programs that sometimes went as high as 30 to 50 percent on sub-contracting. Under Maynard Jackson's leadership, he literally held up the building of the Atlanta airport until there was an adequate number of African American sub-contractors. As mentioned previously, this created 21 millionaires with this one project. The court ruled that African Americans have to prove that there was an intent to discriminate. How do you prove something that is intangible? Many cities including Atlanta have hired consultants and given them large contracts to design programs they feel will withstand the court challenge. Presently there are 240 minority set-aside programs nationwide that are being challenged. Under the leadership of Joshua Smith and the United States Commission on Minority Business Development they have decided this is one of the major areas they are going to monitor along with the Small

Business Administration 8A Program, SBIC and Mesbic Programs, and reduce some of the paperwork in the certification process.

The last area that I want to look at in this chapter is the study Workforce 2000. Some corporate and civic leaders are very much aware that in order for the American economy to remain competitive it can no longer operate on short term goals, but needs to design a long term strategy. Within this context, in the year 2000, 55 percent of the labor force will be people of color. This committee is also aware that by the year 2010, the ratio between workers and recipients will be three to one. The question is will America be able to compete against other countries in the industrialized world including unified Europe, when 42 percent of Black and Hispanic youth 17 years of age can't read beyond a sixth grade reading level? When they have a national dropout rate of 23 percent and in the inner-city 40 percent? Can America compete when it chooses to cut monies for Chapter One and Pell Grants and yet allocates 18 to 38 thousand dollars to prisons knowing that 85 percent of the inmates released return?

An expose' on 'Prime Time Live' showed the poor quality of day care services in America and compared them to Sweden, Japan, and other countries where their day care workers in many cases are required to hold a masters degree. The child to adult ratio is three to one and it is subsidized by the government. America could also subsidize its education if it did not have its money tied up in the military and in prisons.

> Could the reason why Germany, Japan, and other countries subsidize education be because they utilize America's militia to maintain their share of the trilateral commission? I'm very concerned about the richest country in the world being the leader in incarcerating people followed by the Union of South Africa and then the USSR. These are the present conditions that African Americans must face as, we move toward economic empowerment.[15]

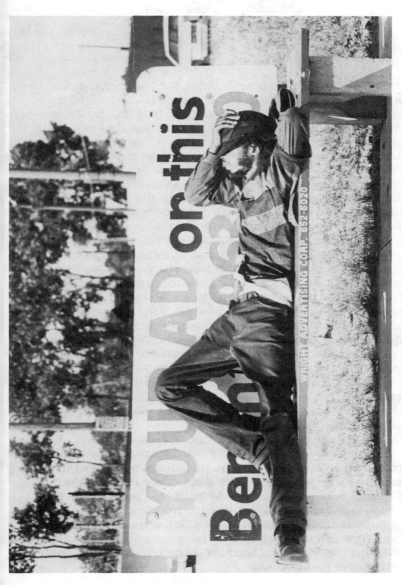

When was the last time the African American community was at full employment?

Chapter 2

The History of Black Economic Development

The history of African economics does not begin in the United States of America. It does not start in 1619, rather, 3.75 million years ago. The first human was recorded to have lived in Africa. The Africa that we will briefly describe in this chapter is not the Africa that Europeans and Arabs invaded and took over 100 million Africans along with much of the mineral resources from countries. Nor, is it the Africa that was divided up among European countries in the 1880s at the Berlin Conference as if they were all sitting down having a piece of pie. The history of economics, as it relates to the Africa that I want to describe, is an Africa with the longest river in the World (The Nile River) and the first agricultural society that resulted from this vast reservoir. It was the richness of "The Nile Valley "and the tremendous number of natural minerals and crops that allowed Africans to build pyramids, temples, and tombs. This Africa unlike the present Africa that suffers from famine and drought had people with the time, energy, and ability to build great monuments; one going on to be one of the seven wonders of the world. It should be obvious to the reader that you could not do this if you were worried about your next meal.

Julius Nyerere in the book, Ujamaa Essays on Socialism states:

We in Africa have no more need of be converted to socialism than we have of being taught democracy. Both are rooted in our past - in the traditional society which produced us. Socialism - like democracy is an attitude of mind. It has nothing to do with the possession or non-possession of wealth. Destitute people can be potential capitalists - exploiters of their fellow human beings. A millionaire can equally well be a socialist; you may value his wealth only because it can be used in the service of his fellow men.

> But the man who uses wealth for the purpose of dominating any of his fellows is a capitalist. So is the man who would if he could. The foundation, and the objective, of African

socialism is the extended family. The true African socialist does not look on one class of men as his brethren and another as his natural enemy.[1]

This is the Africa and its value system that undergirds our economic analysis. A rich land filled with natural minerals and a people that saw themselves as being part of an extended family. This model society did not measure wealth where five percent of the people own nearly 50 percent of the wealth as is practiced in the United States.[2]

Rather, a more equitable distribution of the wealth was employed with little to no homelessness and famine. Major resources that make-up an economy are land and its natural minerals, human labor, and technology. Nyerere has a very concise account of how capitalists view land, one of the major resources of an economy.[3]

In rejecting the capitalist attitude of mind which colonism brought into Africa, we must reject also the capitalist methods which go with it. One of these is the individual ownership of land. To us, in Africa, land was always recognized as belonging to the community. Each individual within our society had a right to use the land because otherwise he could not earn his living. One cannot have the right to life without also having the right to some means of maintaining life. The Africans right to land was simply the right to use it; he had no other right to it. Nor did it occur to him to try and claim one. The foreigner introduced a completely different concept - the concept of land as a marketable commodity. According to this system, a person could claim a piece of land as his own private property, whether he intended to use it or not. could take a few square miles of land, call them mine and then go off to the moon. All I had to do to gain a living from my land was to charge rent to the people who wanted to use it.

This is a fundamental change in how land was viewed in the African economy; land belonged to the extended family. In the capitalist European American economy, land belonged to the individual. This was the first downfall in the African economy. The second downfall was the introduction of money. A means of currency was used in the exchange of goods and services. Exploring our own African history, we understand that services and products were distributed among the people based on a barter system. The Kunjufu family produced yams and the Ofari family produced tomatoes. We exchanged products between each other and this was done without the use of currency. The book by William Griggs, *The Megalite Connection,* describes an African society that for such a long number of years was not dependent on currency. With the introduction of money, people began to horde money. They began to determine people's self-worth based upon the size of their money. People no longer worked if they were not going to receive money. The major components of an economy are land and labor. If land is now owned by the individual, and people are no longer going to function unless they receive some means of currency for their labor, this will then create an economy where people may have time, energy and ability, but they are not going to work if they are not going to receive currency.

In the present capitalistic economy, there are numerous people in America, specifically in the African American community who are not productive, because they are not receiving currency and consequently they are not going to work. In the traditional African society everyone was a worker. We have come a long way from the Nile Valley community to America. In Africa, the land belonged to the entire community, everyone worked and people exchanged goods and services with each other based on a barter arrangement. We now live in an economy where land is owned by individuals, people will not work unless they are hired. Unfortunately, in the African American community, there are people who have never worked and it is projected they will never work and have been reduced down to receiving welfare compensation. There are numerous differences between the traditional African economy and the present European American economy. The major difference between a socialist society and a capitalist society does not lie in their methods of producing wealth, but in the manner that wealth is distributed.

This book will not allow me to go into an in-depth discussion on the merits of productivity and additional compensation. Methods have to be designed not to discourage those with a greater work ethic from becoming complacent. My major contention is the fact that we live in a society where there are people who do not do traditional work, but own the land and/or the means of production and receive a distorted share of the wealth. This inequitable distribution of the assets creates unemployment, homelessness, crime, and the need for more prisons.

The African American community could finance its liberation struggle with a portion of the salaries of its athletes and entertainers who are signing contracts for millions of dollars. Because we have lost our values, we have magazines that glorify 20-bedroom houses shaped like boxing gloves, and all the other capitalistic, materialistic paraphernalia that goes with the people who value external over internal. It is from this African tradition coming out of the Nile Valley, that we now move into America imperialism and slavery. There have been many African Americans who have been able to adjust (as early as the late 1770s) to the American economy; and have become very successful understanding economic principles.

In 1830, there were 3,777 African Americans who were slave owners. It's a very complex point that some Africans bought slaves for their protection. Unfortunately, there were Africans who bought slaves only for their own personal greed and exploitation. Paul Cuffe is a shining example of an African American who in spite of slavery and all of its injustices between the period of 1779 and 1818 was actively involved in Black economic development.

> Cuffe learned the industry of shipping and sailing. He owned six ships, transported several thousand Africans to their homeland, contributed to many worthwhile causes, and challenged the American judicial system on whether African Americans should pay taxes when they were not allowed to vote. During this period, he met with president James Madison and leading White business merchants. He was the richest African American of his time.[4]

In Philadelphia, in 1800 African Americans had accumulated $250,000 worth of assets and owned two insurance companies. This is absolutely amazing because this was during slavery! In 1840, Cincinnati's total wealth of African Americans living in that city was $109,000. In New York City, that same year, the total wealth was $854,000. Please also note that these dollar figures have not been adjusted for inflation.

Black economic development is not a novice idea. As early as 1853, an economic convention took place in Rochester, New York. Martin Delaney was involved in much of the coordination of this conference and the slogans 'Buy Black' and 'Double Duty Dollars' began at conventions like this. In 1865, Tommy Lafon from New Orleans, had accumulated a personal wealth of $413,000. Steven Smith had accumulated $500,000. In 1865, the federal government via the Freedom Bureau created the Freedom bank. Seventy thousand African Americans became depositors in this bank that lasted approximately nine years. Frederick Douglass was appointed chairman of the board to try to create trust among African Americans to deposit their monies together. It's been reported that during this same year, the African American community had accumulated $50,000,000 dollars in assets. Compare this accumulation of wealth (add inflation to that) to monies that we're making today. There's no comparison that our ancestors understood economic development much better than we understand it in the 21st Century.

> In 1889, we conceived a second bank and our first privately owned bank in the state of Virginia. In 1890, it's reported that we had already started 31,000 businesses. In 1898 under the leadership of Booker T. Washington and Fred Moore there was a convention in Atlanta that spearheaded the development of the National Negro Business League. At this convention, the concept of "Buy Black" and "Double Duty Dollars" was greatly reinforced.[5]

Within that same year of 1898, one of the largest Black insurance companies was founded in Durham: North Carolina Mutual Insurance. This city in North Carolina has a rich history with which African American People are not greatly familiar. The founders of North Carolina Mutual were John Merrick, a barber who had no formal education and Dr. Aaron McDuffy-Moore, a Black physician. This was an excellent combination and it reinforced the values taking place in Durham where there was less division between the haves and the have nots. African Americans today need to learn the importance of networking between those possessing degrees in business and 'lay' people who understand the streets. If we could blend people with skills and guts together, much of the $300 billion that we spend elsewhere could stay within the African American community. This combination of John Merrick and Dr. Moore went on to develop the Mechanics and Farmers Bank in 1908 and invested funds in North Carolina Central College. One of the Black financial leaders greatest achievements was the development of the Hayti Business District into a business section of the Black community. Hayti, named after the Republic of Haiti, was fully developed by the turn of the century. Although most of the businesses began life in simple wood-framed buildings, funding continued rapidly and by 1910, Hayti had become a well established business section.

Durham's Black owned banks actively recruited perspective entrepreneurs and brought economic development into the area by providing business and property loans that were unavailable from White institutions. The diversity of goods and services were so wide-ranging in Hayti, that Black residents could meet most of their needs by patronizing establishments. At its peak, Hayti would accommodate 150 thriving Black businesses.[6]

A glowing tribute to these institutions is the fact that not one of them fell during the Depression. This achievement is a testament to the cooperation of the community and the sound advice and financial assistance the Mechanics and Farmers banks were able to provide. Elijah Muhammad, Malcolm X, and Louis Farrakhan all advocated economically that one should move to do for self. Other races have developed an economic base and have hired politicians to represent and reinforce their economic interest. For some reason, African Americans want to build the political base before the economic foundation.

In 1900, African American businesses had increased nationally to 40,000. In 1908, we moved from one federal bank to 55 privately owned banks[7]

In 1912, we had our first millionaire (R. R. Church) who made his fortune in real estate.

Another city with a rich tradition was Tulsa, Oklahoma. The African American community only numbered 11,000 in 1923. This small economically conscious African American community had nine hotels, 19 restaurants, and 31 grocery stores and meat markets.

In terms of professionals, they had 10 medical doctors, six lawyers, and five real estate and loan insurance agencies. Whites called this community "Little Africa." The African Americans referred to their community as "Greenwood." [8]

17

Booker T. Washington was a strong advocate of Black economic development. Washington advocated skill development such that in 1903, in Durham there were 110 African American brick masons compared to 15 Whites. By 1929, these numbers had changed from 85 to 150 respectively.[9]

This was a result of Whites realizing how lucrative the trades were, institutional racism, and African Americans becoming more desirous of white collar professions. Unfortunately, many of our present day scholars have viewed Booker T. Washington as a "Tom" and yet Booker T. Washington motivated Marcus Garvey to come to America and take advantage of building an economic base.

Garvey arrived in America in 1916. His mentor, Booker T. Washington, had died but he stayed in America and went on to develop the Black Star Line Factories Corporation, UNIA, and several other businesses including a newspaper called *Negro World*. Marcus Garvey raised $950,000 for his diverse business ventures. Madame C. J. Walker also became a millionaire during this period. She made her million from responding to a need.

Unfortunately, it was that African Americans wanted to change the texture of their hair to emulate the texture of their oppressor. In 1925, African Americans had developed 103,870 businesses. There was a 300 percent increase in Black owned businesses between 1904 and 1929.[10]

This period was also one of the most volatile periods in race relations and the entrenchment of "Jim Crow" laws. These Black codes were the major catalyst for African American business formation due to segregation. It created in the African American community a concept called an "enclave".

This kind of enclave or community creates a situation where African Americans are dependent on each other both as providers and consumers. The lack of competition from White businesses helped to stimulate growth during this period. In contrast to our present situation with integration the lack of loyalty in supporting Black businesses, the ability for African American consumers to drive 20 and 30 miles away from their own businesses, and African merchants encouraging people to buy Black regardless, of quality and price and service has made it very difficult for us, in the 21st century, to develop economic enclaves like we had in Durham and Tulsa.

In most cities, 70 percent of the businesses within our community are not owned by African Americans. This was not the case during one of the zeniths of Black business development. The last major contributor that I want to add to this period of Black economic history is the Nation of Islam that was formed in 1934. The honorable Elijah Muhammad worked with Marcus Garvey and understood the economic principles that Marcus Garvey and Booker T. Washington espoused. He developed the Nation of Islam and one of the major tenets was economic development. In every city that the Nation opened up a mosque, they also attempted to establish food stores, restaurants, bakeries, and clothing stores. They developed a newspaper, *"Muhammad Speaks"*. In the latter years, they began to distribute Whiting fish and also embarked on the production and distribution of Power products. The Nation of Islam also acquired land for the ultimate production of food that can be distributed to the inner-city. This chronology of Black economic history beginning in 1779 with Paul Cuffe and going through 1934 with Elijah Muhammad is something that needs to be carefully studied and appreciated for the ability to confront slavery, lynchings, and Jim Crow laws and to participate in a capitalistic economy initially with no capital. John Butler has written an excellent book titled *Entrepreneurship and Self-Help Among Black Americans* which chronicles the history of Black businesses and describes their self-determining spirit.

This economic development came in spite of the fact that in 1844, the license of a Black innkeeper was revoked in Virginia without explanation. Financial growth occurred although in 1852, a Maryland law denied Blacks membership in building a homestead association and investing in banks. The African American community flourished economically, even though White mobs in Cincinnati burned down a successful Black furniture business and continued to burn it down after it had been rebuilt three different times. The African American economic shores withstood the tide when little Africa, in Tulsa, Oklahoma was destroyed because a Black man accidentally touched a White female in an elevator.

The rumor spread that he raped her. The larger White community wanted to kill the arrested Black man. However, the African American community in Tulsa defended the Black man, who was by this time in jail. There was a mob scene that quickly worsened and the White community went on to burn down the entire Greenwood district. Fifty people were killed and over 1,000 homes and businesses were in ruins. [11]

The African American community has always struggled for freedom. Some led slave revolts while others participated in the economic system. Africans in America have come a long way from the Nile Valley, almost four million years ago, to the 21st Century. The economic system has greatly changed from Ujamaa (cooperative economics), where land belonged to the community and everyone worked in exchange for goods and services. The economy then operated on a bartering scheme versus the present currency system. Africans in America, through the works of Cuffe, the organizers of the (1853) economic conference in Rochester, Booker T. Washington and the National Negro Business League, the founders of North Carolina Mutual Insurance, Marcus Garvey, and Elijah Muhammad attempted to learn economics in America. Africans ability to make the adjustment from cooperative economics to capitalism has been a very difficult one for the masses. Individual success stories of African Americans becoming millionaires cannot negate the large numbers that live below the poverty level and this is why today some African Americans advocate reparations.

It does not appear that America, under a capitalist system, where someone must be exploited, is in the best interest of all African people. Africans were promised by the Freedom Bureau between 1865 and 1870 that they were going to receive 40 acres of land, $50.00, and a mule. Many people often drop the $50.00.

This promise has never been paid. In 1982, the International Tribunal on reparations calculated that the number of African Americans that were slaves and the number of hours they were worked between 1619 and 1865, creates a debt of 4.1 trillion dollars plus inflation and interest. [12]

Many people who have not read U.S. history feel that this claim is unsubstantiated. They feel that America has never designed programs to benefit select groups. White liberals would have us to believe that the work ethic has been the only way that people have been able to achieve success in America. But really, where would America be had it not stolen the land from the Native Americans? Where would America be had it not stolen Africans from Africa and forced them to work in America from 1619 to 1865 for free?

Where would America and Western Europe be if they had not robbed Africa of much of its natural resources? Where would Firestone be if it had not tricked Liberia into a 99 year arrangement of being able to buy a million acres of land for six cent per acre, and being able to choose exactly what land they wanted to buy?[13]

Where would some Whites be if their grandparents had not received the Land Redemption Act in 1841, from which families received 160 acres of land for $1.25 per acre? Where would they be without the Homestead Act of 1862, which gave them 162 acres of land at no charge, coincidentally, right before slavery ended.[14]

Almost two million White families took advantage of this generous offer. Maybe, if White liberals and conservatives voluntarily gave up their inheritance checks from monies received from these acts and slave labor, then we would not need to advocate for reparations.

The position on reparations is well grounded. In 1831, the Supreme Court chose to establish the "domestic dependenation" for the Native Americans. This was designed to provide new territories and a government for the Indian nation. The United States government must provide money and land through the Indian Claims Commission. In 1973, Alaska natives placed a land claim against the U.S. Government, from which they received over a billion dollars and a title to 40 million acres of land. In 1945, the United States, after World War II, financially assisted West Germany, Japan, Bulgaria, Finland, Hungary, Italy, and Romania with the Marshall and MacArthur plan. Also, in this same year, the United States gave the Jews 130 billion gold marks because of the Holocaust. In 1983, the city of San Francisco voted to give Japanese American victims $1,250 per year.

In 1984, mayor Tom Bradley of Los Angeles publicly apologized to the city employees, who were forced to resign and sent to internment camps. The city council gave each of them $5,000 as a token of reparation. In 1987, Congress voted to give each victim $20,000. At a Black economic conference in Detroit in 1969, it was spelled out in clear detail that Africans wanted 200 million dollars for land, 40 million dollars for the development of a bank, 40 million dollars to develop publishing companies, 30 million dollars to develop a research center, 10 million dollars for a training center, twenty million dollars for defense, 20 million dollars for international relations, 40 million dollars for a national television station, and 130 million dollars for a university.[15]

The major question that we need to ask ourselves is Is it in the best interest of all African American people? Very few of our leaders ask this question, therefore, very few solutions are designed for the collective. On the other hand, I have problems with theoreticians who critique every proposal that does not save the entire race and who offer no alternatives. I am not naive enough to believe that if all African Americans were as industrious as Paul Cuffe, Madame C.J. Walker and so many others that poverty would be eradicated. At the same time, I also am not naive enough to believe that any time soon America is going to provide reparations; regardless of historical precedence, the fact it is due to us, and because of the work we rendered to make this country rich. I believe that racism has been at its greatest when it's directed toward people with the most melanin. I'm not very confident that any time soon America is going to grant us forty acres, $50.00, a mule, $20,000, or 4.1 trillion dollars plus inflation and interest.

As you may have guessed, I am not an advocate of capitalism for many reasons. Capitalism requires that the owner accumulates a degree of capital. Europeans advocated a strong work ethic, yet accumulated their capital by taking the land from the Native Americans, people and natural resources from Africa and using them to create wealth. I call this accumulation "Old Money." Generations upon generations of White Americans have been taking advantage of "Old Money." It doesn't take much ability to receive 160 acres of land at $1.25 per acre, or 162 acres free of charge, or to use other people to work for you and to take their resources and make millions upon millions of dollars. If an illiterate person born into a family that starts off with 20 million dollars in the bank keeps the money in a pass book account, the family would remain rich. Therefore, my first criticism of capitalism is that again it requires the accumulation of capital. African Americans have no desire to take land from anyone or use other people to work for them or take their natural resources. Thus, the only way to acquire capital would be through reparations, a progressive loan policy for African Americans, pooling of economic resources within the African American community, and greater support of African American businesses.

The second problem with capitalism is that while the work is done cooperatively, the profit returns back to the individual that possess the capital. There are only three ways to operate a business: at a loss, break even and at a profit. Socialists and Nationalists have real problems with the term "profit." If we operate a business at a loss, what benefit will there be to the larger African American community as that business becomes bankrupt? If the business breaks even, where would the growth come from to create new products and employ additional people? The only way to produce additional products and employ additional people is with the excess between revenue and cost. If this excess is used for the collective good of the community, then I think that's an advantageous position for the African American community.

The third major concern with capitalism is whether Africans can employ all of the members of the African American community. I'm not impressed with five percent of our community being able to live lavishly and being portrayed in television shows and magazines, and "making it" in America, while one-third of our race lives below the poverty level. At the same time, I am very pleased that our company has been able to employ close to 100 people. I'd rather have made that contribution than to be sitting on the sidelines criticizing people for not coming up with a solution that would employ 40 million people. I think that we all have a responsibility to do whatever we possibly can to put our people back to work. In the next chapter, "Why Foreigners Do So Well," we will illustrate the influx of foreigners, and its implications for the African American community.

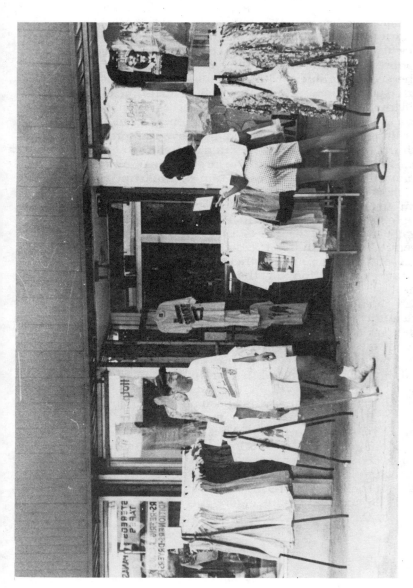

How have foreigners made a profit in a under-developed community?

Chapter 3

Why Foreigners Do So Well

As you walk down Lenox Avenue on 125th street in New York, Cottage Grove in Chicago, Crenshaw Boulevard in Los Angeles, Broad Street in Philadelphia, and Rosa Parks Boulevard in Detroit, it makes you wonder if you're in the African American community or the United Nations.

> Welcome to International Boulevard where every ethnic group is allowed in and everyone is also allowed to take our money out. The business ownership ratio per thousand is 107 (Lebanese), 93 (Syrians), 89 (Koreans), 65 (Japanese), 64 (Whites), 60 (Chinese), 30 (Columbians), 21 (Jamaicans), 17 (Hispanics), and 9 for African Americans. [1]

Movies have been produced such as "Do The Right Thing" that illustrate foreigners conducting business within the African American community while the indigenous population stands on street corners wondering what happened and what really is the right thing to do. Many cities are embroiled in controversy over disputes and fights between foreign merchants and African American customers. Numerous arguments take place over the lack of communication and respect given to the community, and a sense of frustration sets in. It is really sad to observe African American men who live in a community all their lives and end up on a corner while, Asians and Arabs come off a boat, and open up stores in the heart of the African American community.

What is the right thing to do? Talk about them from across the street? Support their businesses? Open our own stores? Burn their stores down? Learn from them? Picket around their stores? Support other Black businesses? What is the right thing to do?Numerous incidents have taken place nationwide illustrating that many of these stores have higher prices, oftentimes unsanitary conditions, and are designed more like prisons than stores with most of the items behind the counter and you point to the item of your choice. Sometimes there is even verbal abuse.

A recent incident took place in Chicago in an African American community, where the residents were very frustrated at the poor service and quality they were receiving from the foreign merchants. There seemed to be a great degree of turmoil. Proposals were circulating about picketing and boycotting the store. It became a very lively discussion on a radio talk show. However, a White merchant called in and said, I don't know why the African American community is upset because if those people leave who will feed and clothe you? He went on to say that he was a former merchant in that same community, but grew tired of the declining profits, crime, and increasing costs due to security and insurance. He again raised the question, Where are the African Americans that will replace the foreigners?

Before the caller's comment, all the phone lines were lit and people were calling in with their story of how poorly they had been treated in many of the foreign businesses, but after this caller raised the question, the phone lines became open and the host had to go to a commercial break. It was obvious they wanted to discuss the poor service they were receiving from foreign businesses, but when challenged with the major question, if foreigners did not come in to the African American community to feed and clothe them, what would they do? The conversation ceased.

There are numerous myths about the success of foreigners operating businesses within the African American community. Many of these myths are believed by the people on the corner, the working class community, and even within the educational community. There are misconceptions about the success of Arabs, Asians, and others in the African American business community. One of the more popular myths is access to low interest loans from banks, and the tremendous profitability of their business. Let's take a look at the first perception: that foreigners have easier access to credit from lending institutions than the indigenous population. I've had the opportunity to interview several of the leading Black bank's loan officers and have been able to discuss their loan portfolios and foreigners were not well represented and definitely did not receive lower interest loans. They did confirm that Asians, Arabs and even Africans born in the West Indies form credit associations among each other. In the last chapter on Economic Empowerment, we're going to talk about this as a strategy for success. This is a pooling of economic resources for greater capital formation.

Many of these groups have credit associations with different names. The Chinese call it Fui, the Japanese; SuSu, the Yoruba; Esusu, and Jamaicans; Fufu. In New York City, one third of the businesses owned by Africans are owned by Africans from the Caribbean and yet they constitute only ten percent of the African population.[2]

Oftentimes, we say that this is due to racism, yet it is very difficult to explain how Africans from the Caribbean that look like us are able to start their businesses and do reasonably well. One of the major reasons for this is the utilization of their culture that encourages cooperation.

In the movie "Do The Right Thing," three unemployed African American men were hanging on a corner, wondering how foreigners were able to come in and start their own businesses. The myth starts that they're able to come off the boat with limited English proficiency, and immediately meet with a banker who provides them with income statements and balance sheets from prior U.S. business experiences. They will present to a U.S. banker collateral to warrant receiving $100,000 at a lower interest rate. That's the kind of myth that exists within the African American community. This perception is easily digestible rather than toiling over the possibility that these people came over here, pooled their resources together, and opened up a grocery store, restaurant, or cleaners not from low interest loans, but from a rotating credit association.

The brothers who were sitting on a corner in the movie had just demonstrated how it could be done, when they pooled their resources together for a bottle of wine. I've seen brothers not only put their quarters together for liquor, but graciously share the bottle with all the brothers who are on the corner with them. How unfortunate that this same cooperative spirit does not exist when it's time to place $100 or $1000 on the table per person and cooperatively work together to open a business.

The second popular myth is the high profitability many people feel foreigners make in the African American community. When I listen to many of these talk shows, the impression is given that one of the most lucrative businesses in the entire country is to do business within the African American community. I thought it was very interesting when a White business owner who was former merchant in the African American community pointed out that the reason why he left was because of low profits, higher costs, the need for greater insurance, and concern for his own safety. If doing business in the African American community is so lucrative, why are not more merchants attracted to it? If profits are more than adequate, why does it not allure more White businesses to it and motivate African American businesses to enter?

> Could the answer lie in the reality that the African American middle class has virtually abandoned the inner city with 25.6 percent residing in the suburbs? Or choosing to work for the government or corporate sector? Could it be the decline in retail establishments from 29 percent in 1969 to the present low of 15.6 percent?[3]

Could this reinforce Timothy Bates' analysis that African American professionals are moving away from the "traditional" retail firm, establishing "emerging" service and wholesaling businesses, which now exceed 60 percent, and are positioning them in the central, outlying, or suburban business district - not the inner city? Enterprise Zone legislators may not be cognizant that they may be unsuccessful at attracting African Americans back to the community that nurtured them. Could it be that first generation foreigners, with limited options due to language and lack of U.S. education, enter the only field available - retailing in the poorest U.S. community? This reminds me of a sports team sending its best half to play another team, while leaving its least gifted to play the best foreign team. The Black middle class could learn from the U.S. Olympic basketball team that has now decided the next time they play the Russians, they'll play their best.

High profits may be a myth especially when you begin to interview, as I have, many foreign business owners, not only in their establishments, but in their homes and witnessed an extended family of 12 to 20 people who all work and live together. I've even observed merchants whose store is on ground level and their apartment above. In many of their home countries, like Japan and South Korea, the density of the population is great and many of them are accustomed to having large numbers of people in a small geographical area. One of the excellent ways to create additional capital is to have some of your workers live together and not require additional income for rent.

In a typical African American family of two parents and three grown children, you may have four separate residences and each of the renters paying $500 a month. If three of these rents could be saved over the course of a year, that's $1,500 a month times 12, that generates a total source of capital of $18,000. It becomes endless in terms of possibilities, if in this small example of only three people saving their rents generated that level of capital. Many people who talk about the success of foreigners fail to mention that they not only pool their money together, but also live together and oftentimes live on the premises of the establishment. In addition, the myths don't include the 12, 14, and 16 hour work days. Any entrepreneur will tell you there's a greater chance for profitability when you reduce expenses and increase productivity.

One of the major complaints that the African American community has of foreign businesses is they do not hire as many African Americans as the community feels they should. I wonder am I viewed as racist as president of African American Images choosing to hire my wife, children, and members of my family, community, and church before I make the positions open to foreigners. Beyond just the issue of practicality and proximity, you tend to hire people that you see everyday who are related to you, before you make it public through the local newspaper. Why would anyone want to hire someone who only works 40 hours a week and requires paid overtime and a higher salary than someone who is willing to work six and seven days a week up to 16 hours for a lower salary? It's simply not good business.

Many people also are not aware that while Asians may be foreigners in America, they often possess a great degree of education in their home country. Fifty-nine percent of all Asians who started their businesses in America possess a college degree, 35 percent of White business owners are degreed, and only 27 percent of African American business owners hold degrees. Twenty-two percent of African Americans do not even possess a high school diploma.[4]

This social capital, the possession of critical thinking skills, business acumen, and a community that encourages business formation; I often feel is more significant than financial capital. While many of these foreigners lack english proficiency, they are very astute. This social capital has been very beneficial to the foreign community. The combination of education, rotating credit associations, long hours, and living together has created for many a very profitable enterprise. It has often been said that foreigners, who just entered the United States, seem to come to America knowledgeable of the buying patterns of the African American community. They seem to know what products, prices, colors, sizes, and quantity will be desirable and effective in the African American community.

It disappoints me that for the past 25 years, African merchants have been trying to encourage our youth to buy items with an African motif. Because they were handmade, the price was prohibitive for many people. Foreigners can mass produce similar items overseas and sell them to African American youth very cheaply. On the one hand, I'm very pleased that our youth are now interested in wearing African medallions, caps that have the continent on them, and items that are Africentric, but it is ironic and disappointing that these African items say made in Japan and South Korea. Unfortunately, that is capitalism at its finest: where consumers have a demand for a certain product at a certain price and if a business can supply that, then they will be successful. I simply look at it as a challenge to the African American business to see if they can produce the product competitively in the States, or utilize the resources of our home Africa where labor is also cheap, and we too can make those products inexpensively.

> In the area of financial capital, the average Asian starts a business with $28,300, Whites start with $24,100, and the average African American starts with $11,500. The failure rate for White and Black businesses is 20 and 30 percent higher respectively than for Asian businesses.[5]

Another very interesting aspect of foreigners doing business in the African American community is the concept of an enclave. Earlier, in the chapter on the history of African businesses the concept of an enclave was noted. John Butler in his book *Entrepreneurship and Self-Help Among Black Americans* describes the success in Tulsa, Durham, Chicago, and many cities in the country where African Americans made enclaves successful. Segregation brought benefits and disadvantages, while enclaves are positive by motivating the community to do business with each other. Unfortunately, while foreigners were allowed to develop enclaves, African Americans are seldom allowed to establish businesses in other ethnic group's communities. This restriction, Butler calls an **"economic detour."** African Americans have been the only group in America that had to operate under these "Apartheid" conditions. If Africans earn $300 billion a year, that also becomes the maximum business income. I do not want to belittle how significant that is especially when presently African American businesses are only receiving seven percent of their $300 billion.

One of the issues we will be discussing in the last chapter will be the need to maintain more of that income in the African American community. The point that's being made here about the success of foreigners is that they understand that their market is very limited with the enclave prototype. What makes the foreign model significant enough that I allocated a chapter to it is that they have moved beyond the enclave theory and have created goods and services that are needed outside of their community. They've created an income base that's not restricted to the size of their population and income and therefore their income becomes unlimited if numerous groups have a demand for their product.

> If Chinese only sold chinese food to each other their income would be greatly restricted, but if they can sell their food to African, Hispanic, and European Americans, then they have gone beyond the enclave theory and have now become international business partners. Asians then turn their monies over nine times in their communities, Whites turn over their monies eight times, and we only turn monies over twice in the African American community.[6]

It is important for corporations like individuals to assess themselves and determine what their strengths, economic weaknesses, and talents are and find ways to take economic advantage of those resources. Asians have developed commodities and taken them to the world table for consumption. They also have excelled in the cleaning profession. African Americans have to ask themselves what are our strengths, weaknesses, talents, and what products and services can we export to the international community that we can use for our collective benefit? It has been said that Africans strength is soul food, sports, and music. We have people within our race who are in great demand and are paid very well. As was mentioned in the previous chapter, Africans can literally finance their entire liberation struggle off the economic resources of our entertainers and our athletes. Unfortunately, because we do not see ourselves as a people, then when our stars sign million dollar contracts they sign them for themselves and see very little need to contribute to the larger community.

Can you imagine a basketball game without African Americans playing? Can you imagine a concert without African Americans singers, dancers, and instrumentalists? Can you imagine the field of sports and music without the African American contribution? Those are two of our strengths that unfortunately the race collectively receives very little benefit. We must look at other resources, products, and services which we have and can produce that are in demand by the larger business community so that we not only find ways to secure a greater percentage of our 300 billion dollars, but which will enable us to become business partners in the international community. We must begin to participate in the three trillion dollar global economy. Just as the Chinese ship chop suey, and Italians export pizza into the African American communities for consumption, African Americans need to ship soul food or some other product or service to the global community for consumption.

Foreigners also seem to understand the importance of land. They understand that money can be made in a factory, but there is no additional land being made. One of the first things foreigners seem to do when they come to America, besides knowing the product line needed to be successful in the African American community, is to own the building in which they operate. Eventually, they begin to acquire additional buildings on the block. Many African American businesses have operated in the community for years and have seen their rent spiral over that period of time. Some have never pursued owning the property to maintain some degree of autonomy. Many times when African Americans begin to boycott and picket foreign businesses, they begin contemplating opening up their own businesses, they quickly find out that foreigners have bought the entire block and control the rents. I have witnessed many African American businesses close because the properties were bought by foreigners, who increased the rent for the sole purpose of being able to bring in additional family members to start more businesses. It obviously takes additional capital to acquire a building. It also requires the foresight and social capital to realize that beyond pooling $25,000 to $30,000 to acquire inventory, we also need to continue this rotating credit association and invest another $50,000 to a $100,000 to buy the building.

It is true that bankers do look favorably on lending money in a situation where there's a building that costs a $100,000 and somebody's willing to put down 50 percent in collateral instead of the usual 10 to 20 percent. There are many authors, including Thomas Sowell and Shelby Steele that consistently like to compare Asians and Arabs and even our own brothers and sisters from the Caribbean to African Americans. The fallacy in the argument is comparing immigrants to slaves. Numerous studies point out that you don't compare someone whose culture is intact, people who possess strong self-esteem which can lead to a strong entrepreneurial spirit, with a people whose culture has been denied them, where their self-esteem has been reduced and where they have been, for a long period of time, not only legally denied the opportunity to be an employer, or an employee, but were required to be slaves.

I believe the major asset foreigners bring to America and specifically in the African American community is their culture. A culture that: (1) teaches them to see themselves as a people, as a collective, and not as individuals; (2) encourages them to share their resources together; (3) urges them to pool their economic resources together to start their businesses and to acquire additional properties; (4) impels them to work long and hard and to consider long term gratification at the expense of every one purchasing a Cadillac and a condominium the first year; (5) has the accent on being employers rather than employees and producers rather than consumers; (6) and encourages an entrepreneurial spirit, to study business principles and develop a product or a service that will be demanded in the international market.

In this chapter, I have attempted to describe the impact foreigners have had on the African American community. In the next chapter, "The Global Economy," I will show the interrelationship of the African American community to the world.

Chapter 4

The Global Economy

U.S. Steel has a slogan which states, "As the Nation Goes So Goes the Steel." General Motors had a slogan which stated, "What's Good for Our Country is Good for General Motors and Vice-Versa." Life was very simple 30 to 40 years ago. You either bought a Ford, Chevy, or Chrysler. You either bought ice cream in three flavors: vanilla, chocolate, or strawberry. Now, there are 755 cars to choose from and you can now buy ice cream in 31 to 33 different flavors. This change, this complexity has created an inter-network of corporations and countries, and creating a global economy where companies no longer feel that their borders are restricted by their respective country. This global economy does not restrict corporations to be loyal to citizens of the country in which the corporation is headquartered.

> The Trilateral Task Force report of 1977 said that the public and leaders of most countries continue to live in a mental universe which no longer exists - a world of separate nations - and have great difficulty thinking in terms of global perspective and interdependence.[1]

> Gilbert Williamson of the NCR corporation stated, "I was asked the other day about United States competitiveness and I replied that I don't think about it at all. We at NCR think of ourselves as a globally competitive company that happens to be headquartered in the United States."[2]

These two statements are in extreme contrast with the statements from U.S. Steel and GM. In years past, companies had tremendous loyalty to the country in which they were doing business, but in the global economy there are no restrictions in respect to geography and loyalty. Each company views the entire world as its market. This has major implications for citizens from each country that still naively believe that companies have a responsibility to provide jobs for them in their country. It is obvious that companies do not see it that way. Companies see that they have an obligation to make profits.

This new economy has corporations (global webs) involved in many countries and it is very difficult to determine where a product is actually made. Is the criteria based on where it was finished, where it was financed, or where the raw materials originated? Is it based on engineering or research and development? Let me give an example of it's complexity. The great American company publishes books. The author lives in England; editorial offices are in America; typesetting is done in Hong Kong; illustrations are done in France; printing is done in Japan; marketing and advertising are done in Switzerland; financing is handled in Germany; travel arrangements for a publicity tour for the author are handled in London; and distribution of the books is handled in Canada. What is the American corporation? Is this an American product? What criteria is used to determine that it is an American product? Was it based solely on the fact that the company is incorporated in the United States? Was it determined based on the fact that the book was edited in the United States? All the other contributing factors to the book were done in other countries.

When Americans buy a Pontiac LeMans from General Motors, they engage unwittingly in an international transaction. Of the $20,000 paid to GM, about $6,000 goes to South Korea for routine labor and assembly operations. Thirty-five hundred dollars goes to Japan for advance components (engines, transaxels and electronics). Fifteen hundred dollars go to Germany for styling and design engineering. Eight hundred dollars go to Taiwan, Singapore, and Japan for small components. Five hundred dollars go to Britain for advertising and marketing services, and about $100 go to Ireland and Barbados for data processing. The balance, less than $8,000 go to strategists in Detroit, lawyers and bankers in New York, lobbyists in Washington, insurance and health care workers all over the country, and General Motors share holders, most of whom live in the United States, but an increasing number of whom are foreign nationals. Again, is this an American car? What makes it an American car? Because GM has its headquarters in the United States? Most of the labor was done in South Korea. Most of the equipment came from Japan.

The global economy is very complex and it has major implications for Africans all over the world. In 1987 for example, the Hyster Company, an American owned manufacturer of forklifts and truck headquartered in Portland, Oregon, accused several Japanese owned firms of pricing their forklifts sold in America below what they charged in Japan. This prompted the Commerce Department to propose special duties on the forklift imports. In response, Japanese firms began to make forklifts in the United States. Hyster cried foul! They argued that the competing forklifts were still Japanese since many of their parts came from Japan. What Hyster carefully did not reveal however was that its own American forklifts contained even more foreign parts than those they were accusing of being Japanese. What looked like foreign dumping in the United States was in reality nothing more than one global web charging a lower price in the United States for the globally made forklifts that then were charged by another global web.[3]

It is becoming increasingly complex to distinguish an American company from a foreign company and an American product from a foreign product because so many components of the product have been added to it from other parts of the world. Many Americans and politicians have expressed concern about America's security if products sold to the military are made by foreigners. The U.S. government considers a product American if the corporation has its headquarters in America. The reality is that the Pentagon purchases many products where large portions of the work, specifically designing and engineering, have been done in Asia and have been manufactured in the United States. This complexity also expresses itself as it relates to apartheid in South African. The ruling via sanctions--that have been lifted--was that American companies could not operate in South African. It does not negate the possibility that the American company can license a South African company to produce the very product they were producing themselves in South Africa and contribute largely to its product development from other parts of the world.

In 1990, 40 percent of IBM's world employees were foreigners and the percentage was growing. IBM Japan boasted of having more than 18,000 Japanese employees. Annual sales are more than six billion dollars, which made it one of Japan's major exporters of computers. Consider Whirlpool, after cutting its American work force 10 percent by shipping much of its production to Mexico, and buying Dutch owned Phillip's appliance business, Whirlpool employed 43,500 people in 45 countries. Most of them were not Americans. Look at Segate Technology, a California world leader in the production of hard disk drives. In 1990, the company had 40,000 employees, 27,000 of whom worked in South East Asia. All totaled, more than 20 percent of the output of American owned firms was produced by foreign workers outside the United States and the percentage was rising quickly. Overseas capital spending by American corporations accelerated from the early 1980s onward, increasing by 24 percent in 1988 alone. In fact, Singapore's largest private employer was General Electric, which also counted for a large share of that nation's growing exports. Taiwan meanwhile counted AT&T, RCA, and Texas Instruments among its largest exporters. With the opening of Eastern Europe, American corporations steadily had access to workers happy to labor for wages comparable to those earned by workers in the Philippines.

> American owned corporations increased their overseas spending on research and development by 33 percent between 1986 and 1987. This can be compared to its six percent increase in research and development in the United States.[4]

It should become obvious to the reader that it is not only difficult to determine what exactly is made in America but it should become crystal clear that the American corporation has very little commitment to the American worker and has an ultimate loyalty to making a profit in the world-wide arena. In strong contrast, American corporations and the American populous continue to support the position that the U.S. government should protect its borders from foreign exports. This rationale is held for a myriad of reasons. For the American worker, the concern that exports coming into America will close plants in the United States thus creating greater unemployment for them. American corporations feel that exports coming in reduce their profitability.

The desire of the American worker and the American corporation to express to the government to protect its borders from exports on the surface appears to make sense, but because of the inter-woveness of the global economy where so many variables are interrelated it becomes very challenging. For example, If U.S. Steel appeals to the government to protect its borders from the importation of steel, then it creates havoc for automobile companies who will have to use higher priced steel being built in America for its cars. The consequence is that the automobile companies will not be able to compete against foreign imports. They too then will want to have tariffs placed on imports coming in for cars. The cycle continues. This snowball effect can make it very difficult for other corporations i.e., Coca Cola, McDonald's, IBM, and others to export their products to other countries if America denies steel and cars to enter.

Lee Iacocca, president of Chrysler corporation was instrumental in convincing Congress in 1979 to guarantee the Chrysler corporation $1.2 billion in new loans so that they could avoid bankruptcy and continue to make cars in the United States. He helped force a voluntary restraint agreement on Japan's export of cars to the United States. On television commercials he told Americans to abandon their inferiority complex regarding American made autos versus Japanese imports. However, by the start of the 1990s, Chrysler cars contained the highest percentage of foreign made parts of any of the Big Three, including the most complex components like engines and transaxels. In addition, Chrysler owned 12 percent of Mitsubishi Motors, through Mitsubishi, they owned a part of South Korea's Hyundai Motors, both of which supplied Chrysler customers with Dodge Colts, Chrysler Conquests, Dodge Vistas, Eagle Summits, and other vehicles.

> Other American automotive dealers were similarly disengaging from America. By 1990, Ford owned 25 percent of Mazda and both companies owned shares of South Korea's Kia Motors. Not to be outdone, General Motors bought more than 40 percent of Japan's Isuzu which has supplied it with over 300,000 small cars annually. It bought half of South Korea's Daewoo Motors which has supplied another 80,000 cars and then bought 50 percent of Sweden's Saab.[5]

Before we go into more detail with the micro issues and the implications for corporations and individuals, we need to paint the macro picture. This global economy is part of the final frontier of imperialism and monopoly capitalism. Multinational corporations all under the expose' of Trilateralism are administered by 300 of world's most influential people. Trilateralists believe the people, governments, and economies of all nations must serve the needs of multinational banks and corporations. The control of economic resources spells power in modern politics. Leaders of capitalist democracies with economic control allow political power to rest with a few and must resist movements toward a truly popular democracy. In short, Trilateralism is the current attempt by ruling elites to manage the global economy. The elite reside primarily in the United States, Germany, Western Europe, and Japan.

> As I stated earlier, the global economy is run by approximately 300 individuals of which 290 are men from those four major regions of the world. Their concentration of wealth and power is unbelievable and staggering. The four trilateral regions which represent only 10 percent of the world population produces two - thirds of the world's output. Less than two percent of the world's population owns 32 percent of its wealth. General Motors, Exxon, Shell, Ford, Texaco, Standard, and IBM are companies that have larger sales than many countries. Those companies are in the top 60 of all the countries and companies in the world. The chief executive officer for many of these companies receive salaries and stock options equivalent to $4 million a year. The American corporate president receives a salary on the average of 93 times that of the average worker.[6]

All of the top 100 African American corporations that make up the Black Enterprise 100 combined would total $6 billion and this would place them approximately 100th on the Fortune 500. In contrast, General Motors alone in 1990 had sales of a $127 billion. The total sales for Fortune 500 companies alone was $2.1 trillion.

It is important that we understand the terms "multinational companies" and "monopoly capitalism." The objective of the Trilateral Commission is the coordination of these large corporations that created monopolistic conditions in their respective countries to broaden them into multinational companies where the world's natural and human resources are available to be used by them at their discretion. American corporations want American citizens to buy their products that they produced overseas which is inconsistent with the laws of reciprocity, but very consistent with the goals of capitalism and imperialism, which both espouse exploitation at any cost. The American worker is not competing against foreign firms, but against laborers in Singapore, Taiwan, and Mexico where hourly wages may begin as low as 18 cents an hour. This has major implications for the American labor force and specifically for African Americans. In this global economy, how can the American worker compete against a labor force charging 18 cents an hour? This is a major reason for the destabilization of the African American family, specifically the African American male who before this global economy had a low skilled job in a manufacturing plant receiving union wages of $10 to $18 per hour.

Ironically, as the big three automakers abandoned America, Japanese automakers rapidly filled the gap. Between 1987 and 1990 alone, the Big Three laid off 9,063 American workers while the Japanese hired 11,050. In 1990 Sony was exporting audio and video tapes to Europe from its Dolton, Alabama factory and shipping audio recorders from its Fort Lauderdale, Florida plant. Sharp was exporting 100,000 microwave ovens annually from its factory in Memphis, Tennessee. Dutch owned Phillips Consumer Electronics company shipped 30,000 televisions from its Greenville, Tennessee plant to Japan.

> Toshiba America shipped projection televisions from its main plant to Japan. Matsushita transports cathode - ray tubes from Ohio and Honda was laying plans to export 50,000 cars to Japan from Ohio. In all, in 1990, more that a quarter of American exports wore the labels of foreign owned companies and Japanese owned companies alone accounted for 10 percent of U.S. exports. In 1979, foreign investment equalled about two percent of all non-financial corporations in the United States. By 1988, it equalled nine percent and is expected to reach 15 percent by 1995.[7]

In fact American-owned firms were doing so much abroad and foreigners owned so much here that by 1990, American consumers intent on improving the nations trade balance would have done better by purchasing a Honda than a Pontiac Le Mans. What's the difference between an American corporation that makes or buys abroad much of what it sells around the world and a foreign corporation that makes or buys in the United States much of what it sells? While that question may sound theoretical to some, in actuality, if Honda has a plant in Ohio it is more beneficial for the American worker to take advantage of that experience than for the American worker to take pride in Chrysler and its production of cars in Singapore to be exported back to the United States. Nothing is contradictory in a capitalistic and imperialistic economy. One has to wonder how foreign companies can enter the United States where the labor is higher and would be more cost effective than American corporations that felt it was in their best interest to produce overseas. John Krafcik of MIT's International Motor Vehicles Program found that Americans working in Japanese-owned plants could assemble a car in about 19.5 hours which is just a bit more than the 19.1 hours averaged by Japanese workers, but far less than the 26.5 hours average by American workers in American-owned factories.

> After Toyota took over the management of General Motors factory in Freemont, California, in 1984, productivity soared by 50 percent over what it had been under GM's managers. Absenteeism had been as high as 25 percent under GM management, but under Toyota absenteeism fell to four percent. A similar transformation occurred when Japan's Bridge Stone took over FireStone's ailing U.S. tire factories.[8]

Notably, in both instances the work force remained the same. The only pertinent difference was the exchange from American management and capital to Japanese. It should also be mentioned that the Japanese in this situation also increased monies for research and development especially in the training of its workers. In addition to that, the ratio of CEO's salaries to that of factory workers in Japan and in Japanese companies operating in America was ten to one. Where as the ratio in American corporations at home and abroad can be as high as previously mentioned: in U.S. corporations its 93 percent to one. This is very interesting how an American corporate officer with lower profits, less productivity and greater absenteeism can receive a higher salary than others who are more successful.

The interworkings and complexities of the global economy, monopoly capitalism, and multinational companies are usually over the heads of most African Americans who are still trying to understand what happened in Gary, East St. Louis, Detroit, Camden, Chicago, Pittsburgh, and so many other cities with a manufacturing base. Many African Americans really don't understand the complexities and difficulties competing in a monopoly capitalistic environment. The days of the

1920s where an immigrant could come over from Italy and open up a fruit stand and be competitive are very different for the new merchant competing against the larger food chains. Should an African American pay $3 for a gallon of milk at the local African American store when the larger food chain is selling that same gallon milk for $1.69? How can small merchants compete against K-Mart that sells the latest video for $19.95, while the best they could do is to offer it at $29.95?

While writing this particular chapter, I was informed by my movie promoter that while our movie did very well in an Oakland theatre, because of the interrelationship between the studios and theatres (United Artists, Cineplex Odeon, Loews, General Cinema, and AMC), where in many cases they have the same parent company, (i.e., Paramount, Warner Brothers, Columbia, and Universal Pictures). In numerous cities that we have been in our movie has been moved out not because sales were inadequate, but because one of their movies needed to take its spot. Monopoly Capitalism shows its ugly head in numerous instances. There is a slight movement afoot to acquire some theatres in the African American community. The challenge will be that under the rules of monopoly capitalism they have divided the cities and suburbs into zones and a movie that's in one particular zone can not be at another theater in the same zone. It is also difficult for independent stores to compete against stores in large shopping malls where consumers in record numbers are making their purchases. If you look at how most malls are designed, they are anchored by two to three major chains and the entrances to most of the malls are - conveniently and not coincidentally - through the major chain stores.

I'm sure people are wondering how Asian merchants compete favorably in this global economy. In the preceding chapter, we spoke of some of the techniques that foreigners have been able to implement to be profitable such as credit associations for capital accumulation, cooperation, and living together to keep down expenses. In a global economy foreign based companies import inexpensive products from their home countries i.e., Hong Kong, Singapore and Taiwan and sell them in America. African Americans have an excellent opportunity to take advantage of that same network where labor is less expensive in Africa and natural resources are abundant. In order to achieve this goal, African Americans must overcome obstacles discussed in the upcoming chapter.

Should the American consumer be loyal to the American corporation who uses foreign labor?

Chapter 5

Obstacles To Black Economic Development

African American workers only earn 57 percent of White workers' income, this creates a total loss of income equivalent to 186 billion dollars. The average wealth of a White family is $39,000 in comparison to a Black family at $3,200. This creates a disparity in wealth of $695 billion. As a result, Black businesses only received two percent of the total business sales in America thus, creating a $1.3 trillion deficit.[1]

A people that earns $300 billion a year and has the potential of securing business sales of $3 trillion should not have an unemployment problem within its community. There are many Black economists who don't believe in the power of the Black consumer and the Black business. They feel that businesses are marginal at best and that it's going to require the public sector and the Fortune 500 to stimulate growth in the Black community. These people are quick to point out that a large White firm can employ thousands of people and this makes it far more significant than a small Black business. Many of these experts offer these conclusions in spite of the figures that indicate 80 percent of the employment in the economy is coming from the small business community.

The failure rates for Black businesses are significant, within a three year period 30 percent of all Black businesses have failed, within five years 75 percent, and within 10 years 80 percent.[2]

This chapter is an attempt to look at the obstacles to Black economic development including: why we have not been able to keep more of our $300 billion in our community; why our businesses have not been able to generate sales consistent with our total population figures; what can be done to reduce the failure rates of Black businesses; and we will also take an honest look at whether Black businesses can stimulate growth within the community and significantly reduce unemployment.

One of the major obstacles to Black economic develop. ment is the social environment that surrounds starting a Black business. I've noticed in Black families that if there are four adult siblings and three of them are professionals and one is a business owner, among the family, the professionals seem to be revered more than the business owner. I have seen churches, professional organizations and magazines give more credence and recognition to professionals than to business owners. Carter G. Woodson in the book *Miseducation of the Negro* made reference to how schools encourage African Americans to pursue careers working and managing other peoples enterprises versus starting their own. Schools feel that it is more prestigious to be an account- ant for a Fortune 500 corporation than to own a grocery store or cleaners in the community. There is a perception that Black businesses are marginal, require too much work for too little income, and that it's more lucrative, less demanding and more financially rewarding to work for someone else than to own your own business.

In the previous chapter, we talked about the number of businesses per thousand members in a community in the Black, White, Hispanic, and Asian communities. African Americans have the smallest number of busi- nesses per thousand. I think a major reason for this is that the social environment does not encourage people to start businesses. Many of the men and women who do form businesses start them after a great deal of frustra- tion due to not being able to climb the corporate ladder. Some females within our community who have the time, money, and maturity to raise children unfortunately are not having as many as those with the least time, money, and maturity, who are having more children. The same applies in the business community. Many of our best Black minds, who have the degrees in engineering, ac- counting, marketing, and business administration are using their skills and talents for corporate America, while other members of our community who have not been trained in the business community are starting "mom and pop businesses" which reinforces that Black busi- nesses are very marginal.

Many of us underestimate business viability. What we perceive to be a marginal operation in actuality is just the opposite when we total the business receipts for the day, week, month, or year. I still regret that during the Montgomery bus boycott of 1955, our people didn't

nd that after 381 days of creating an alternative
ce, freedom should have also been defined in
terms. We did not need to return back to riding
es that were losing money because of our
Ve should have continued on with the main-
f our own bus system. This is a slave mentality
orting and working for others versus ourselves in
rican American community.

any of us look down on the grocery stores, cleaners,
d "marginal operations" because we lack a vision of
now Ford, GM, Chrysler, IBM, Xerox, and others started
as "marginal operations." We were not there when they
met in the basements of their homes, developing
strategies. We were not there to observe the 12, 16, and
20 hour work days seven days a week. We were not there
when payrolls were missed and financial sacrifices were
made. We were not there when they borrowed money
from relatives because they had a vision that years later
they would have million dollar operations. I will never
forget the day my mother loaned me $1,000 to start
African American Images and how gratifying it is to see
that seed money blossom. It has been said that a people
without a vision will perish and unfortunately, that is
happening in the business sector of our community.

On the other hand, some of our people dream too much
and businesses require more than dreams. They require
hard work, sacrifice, and planning. John Raye from the
Majestic Eagles, makes a distinction between a goal and
a wish: The latter, you never do anything about, the
former, you work on it constantly. Many of our people
are so used to being involved in large corporations that
it's very difficult for them to imagine starting a business
from scratch. As a person who's a strong advocate of
self-esteem, I never want to burst anyone's bubble and
destroy their dream. People come up to me all the time
and tell me about their million dollar dreams. I listen,
but to myself I have major doubts about whether they
have persistence. My desire is to always encourage
people, seldom do I make discouraging remarks. As I
become older, I feel more of a need to at least point out
to people that dreams do require blueprints. Another
obstacle affecting Black economic development within
the business community is the lack of trust. It is very
difficult to do anything in this world by yourself. The
same cooperative spirit that Asians and other im-
migrants have in studying together; they replicate in the

business sector by pooling their resources. This level
trust is necessary if a business is going to be successfu
Prosperous businesses establish and maintain trus
with their customers, workers, and investors. It becomes imperative that if we're going to be successful as
business owners we have to acknowledge that trust is as
essential an ingredient as capital and business acumen.

Another obstacle that affects Black businesses is the
desire to convince themselves, their families, and their
communities that there businesses are viable. This is
demonstrated by the purchase of expensive clothes, cars,
and houses. Many business owners fall prey to
materialism and the desire to refute this image that
Black businesses are marginal by making expensive
purchases. The assumption being that my business can't
be marginal if I'm driving a Cadillac, BMW, or Mercedes.
The reality is those kind of purchases rob a business of

Percentage of (Black) Consumers
Who Buy At:

Types of Goods or Services Bought	Stores Owned By Blacks	Stores Owned By Whites	Total
Groceries	27.9	72.1	100.00
Drug-store purchases	41.1	58.9	100.00
Men's clothing	0.9	99.1	100.00
Women's clothing	1.1	98.9	100.00
Children's clothing	1.0	99.0	100.00
Men's shoes	0.6	99.4	100.00
Women's shoes	0.3	99.7	100.00
Children's shoes	1.0	99.0	100.00
Furniture	2.9	97.1	100.00
Hardware	4.3	95.7	100.00
Other household supplies	15.9	84.1	100.00
Flowers	47.0	53.0	100.00
Automobile repairs	41.8	58.2	100.00
Gasoline, oil, etc.	53.8	45.2	100.00
Shoe repairs	75.0	25.0	100.00
Cleaning and pressing	74.4	25.6	100.00
Tailoring	80.3	19.7	100.00
*(4) All Types	27.6	72.4	100.00

capital for future growth and development. I'm
that Black business owners should take an
verty and never utilize some of their business
for personal pleasure, but I do feel that balance
ation are essential. I recognize that many of
view Black businesses as being marginal and
e opportunity for refutation, but there are other
ives to convincing the larger community that
businesses are viable and need to be pursued. The
k business community and the teaching profession
ed a major public relations campaign to communicate
their tremendous benefits.

Another major obstacle to Black economic development
is the attitude of the Black consumer. I often ask Black
consumers several questions: what is their commitment
to the race, how much value do they place on Black
businesses, and is their loyalty greater than a penny or
a nickel. I heard a horror story recently from a Black
business owner who had been in business for several
years. A foreigner opened up a business and was selling
the same hair care product. His store sold it for $4.99
and the foreigner sold it for $4.95. He told me there was
a marked decline in the sales of this particular product
and that African American customers were telling him
that his prices were too high, only for him to find out that
the difference in price was a mere four cents. Again, I
raise the question, how much loyalty do we have to the
race? Can it be bought for a penny, nickel or dime?

I am not trying to deny that there are oftentimes larger
price disparities between products sold in African
American stores and non African American stores. In the
chapter on the Global Economy, we looked at monopoly
capitalism. Some large chain stores advertise they will
not be underpriced. I am very much aware that a store
that buys a million copies of item X is not going to be
undersold or underpriced by a small African American
store that only bought 100 items. I am saying that
oftentimes, the price differential is much smaller than
sometimes we are willing to acknowledge. The question
remains what price do we place on our loyalty to the race?
People often tell me they support Black stores as long as
Black stores have prices that are lower than non-African
American stores, but if the price becomes equal or if the
price becomes four cents higher their loyalty begins to
wane.

A significant obstacle is the poor service provided by some African American businesses. George Subira states, "Black people start businesses to be the boss and Whites start them to make money."[3]

Due to the enclave theory, some African American businesses assume that because they are Black, they should be supported. Listed below is a table historically describing the response of Black consumers to Black businesses.

Timothy Bates and numerous others have documented that businesses can't assume race loyalty; they must provide quality service. African American businesses can't open late, close early, treat customers rudely, talk on the phone while servicing customers, and have an untidy store that is also understocked.

In the last chapter, Black Empowerment, we will look at strategies that Black businesses can utilize against large White chain stores beyond the issue of price. There are other aspects of business that should be considered before a final decision is made on where you want to purchase and they include: the quality of the product, service, proximity, and community support, etc. I've even heard stories from Black business owners that when foreigners come in, many Black consumers simply wanted to give them a chance. One of the strengths and weaknesses about African people is our desire to be humane, open, honest, and fair. As a result of this, a foreigner can come into the African American community and in our desire to be fair we want to support both businesses. We need a Black consumer base that will be charged with the responsibility of doing whatever they possibly can to stimulate growth within their community. It is a two fold responsibility between Black businesses and Black consumers. We need a consumer base that will drive a little further, be considerate and patient, and understand that supporting Black businesses is supporting themselves. Unfortunately, just as we have no schools that take children from pre-school through college teaching commitment to the liberation struggle, we don't have any schools that teach Black consumers their responsibility to support Black businesses. People often ask, what can I do to aid the Black community? What can I do to assist in the liberation struggle? One of the things that can be done is the support of Black businesses. This does not negate the need for Black businesses to also give back to the community in the way that Black consumers give to them. Ultimately, we will not see ourselves on different sides of the table. We will see ourselves as one family.

Another factor I want to look at that's creating obstacles to Black economic development is the lack of business knowledge to start and run a business successfully. Many businesses in the African American community have been started because people possess product knowledge but not accounting, marketing, and other business expertise. They know how to make fried chicken and sweet potato pie, but they really did not understand marketing, accounting, and taxes. When the failure rate for business is 85 percent within a 10 year period one major area that has to be assessed is the lack of knowledge and business expertise. Numerous businesses in the Black community have failed for no other reason than the fact that they did not pay their taxes. For many, they did not inform the government of their business operations, and led themselves to believe that the government would not find out. However, the government did find out and a large tax liability was assessed, and they were unable to pay. There are other businesses that were officially registered with the government, but because of cash flow problems, did not pay the government and Uncle Sam, unlike landlords, creditors, and employees, doesn't knock on the door immediately expecting payment. Many businesses have found out three, six, or nine months later that when the government finally catches up with them, they expect to receive all their money plus interest and penalty. It is also unfortunate that with such a large number of African American professionals who possess degrees in accounting that we can't find ways to help these business avoid pitfalls. There's a tremendous "Black Brain Drain" in our community where the information is not flowing from those that have to those that need. Product knowledge is not the only aspect of a business that is necessary to be successful. In my study of well run corporations there is a balance between product knowledge or engineering, marketing, and accounting. Successful presidents and CEO's either have worked in all three areas or they have people closely related to them that bring those strengths to the table. A company that has strong expertise in marketing, but has not allocated the proper time, attention, and financial resources to product development, research, and engineering is not going to be stable in the long run. A company that is strong in marketing, but has lax credit and collections policies, and has not secured the data such as cash flow and income statements is not going to be prepared to make sound decisions.

Some of the entrants to the business community are professionals who have a strong expertise in marketing and accounting, but have not produced a product. They are primarily in the service sector, (i.e., real estate, insurance, etc.) little overhead, but limited potential for employment. With an astronomical failure rate for all businesses and specifically African American business, people must make time to review or develop financial records, and attend courses or seminars. Many business programs offered in the community are free or at a nominal charge. We must bridge the gap between those with the guts that started their business, because they could make fried chicken, but have their receipts in a shoe box and those with the skills and business acumen, who presently work downtown, and don't know how to make sweet potato pie. If this gap could ever be bridged, then maybe we could secure the 17 percent of all business sales due to African American community.

> Another major obstacle to Black business development is the lack of credit and capital. Only 10 percent of African American business owners indicate they secured loans from commercial banks as sources of equity.[5]

> African Americans relied almost solely on themselves, while other ethnic groups relied on greater personal wealth, relatives, friends, and banks. As mentioned, the average African American firm has a start-up capital of $11,500, Whites $24,100, and Asians $28,300.[6]

Many people feel that this is the major problem for business development. I feel that this is secondary to the lack of racial understanding between Black consumers and Black businesses. I don't negate that capital is a major obstacle for Black business development and there are numerous factors including discriminating banks and corporations, the lack of Black wealth, and "Negro" banks that are very conservative about their investment portfolios. There are many cities where Black banks don't even exist and the larger banking community has not been very encouraging to African American businesses in the form of capital availability. All the theories and books can't cover up that a major obstacle of Black economic development is institutional racism in the banking industry. There have been loans made to White corporations that had little or no collateral and less sales potential but they secured the loan because of the "buddy buddy" system also called institutional racism.

Oftentimes, businesses could survive if they had an extension of credit from key suppliers. Many people confuse capital with credit. We all have heard about the difficulties for Black businesses because of lack of capital, but we don't hear as much about Black businesses that suffered because of a lack of credit. If Black businesses were able to secure credit from their major vendors for the first 30 to 60 days, it would allow many of them to become stabilized. More studies have been done about the discrimination within the banking industry than from suppliers who often deny Black businesses the opportunity to pay within thirty days. It becomes a "catch 22" when Black businesses pay a vendor in advance for supplies but can't use that track record to secure credit from another vendor because a credit history has not been established. How can a person or business ever be considered a good credit risk until it is extended?

In conclusion, there are many obstacles affecting business formation. We have reviewed the lack of social reinforcement and trust, business liability, consumer and business attitudes, acumen, and lack of capital and credit. In the remaining chapters, we will outline what individuals, businesses, and communities can do to overcome these obstacles.

Chapter 6

The Responsibilities of Being an African American Consumer

In the introduction, I mentioned that one of the major objectives of this book was to increase the number of African American owned businesses. Our present numbers are nine African American businesses per 1000. The White community has 64 businesses per 1000. In reality even if we increase our numbers from nine to 64 we would still have 936 people in our community that were not businesses owners - but consumers.

Another objective indicated in the introduction was to develop a community of consumers to become more economically literate. This chapter is designed to build personal wealth. The African American community needs consumers that are economically knowledgeable and committed to the overall development of its own community.

In a typical four-corner intersection in the African American community there will be a storefront church, a barbecue house, and two liquor stores. This is a community that has one third of its residents suffering from high blood pressure and heart disease. This four corner scenario is not the most efficient way to develop the African American economy. A typical scenario in our community with two liquor stores, is one owned by a foreigner and the other owned by an African American. They are both selling a pint of wine for 99 cents. Foreigners i.e., White, Arab, Korean, and Jewish know most African American consumers are more concerned about price than racial loyalty. Consequently, they understand that a reduction in price will increase their sales. Therefore, they lower the price from 99 cents to 69 cents, and as predicted the African American consumers increase their sales with the foreign business. Very few African American consumers will inquire from the African American business owner why their prices are higher than the foreign establishment. If they had done so, the African American business owner could have informed the customer that there is a price war going on with an attempt to eliminate the competition, creating only one liquor store on the corner. Unfortunately, the African

American business owner also did not call a meeting or inform the public with fliers that a price war had ensued. This lack of communication between the African American consumer and business owner stimulates foreign business. The African American enterprise becomes bankrupt and with only one liquor store on the corner the new price of wine is no longer 69 or 99 cents, but now it retails for $1.29. It is also very possible that a new African American merchant will open a liquor store within the next couple of years, but without the above historical knowledge the same scenario will unfold. An objective that we would like to establish in this chapter is for African American consumers to communicate more with African American merchants and vice-versa. It will be very difficult for us to curtail the foreign invasion of our community without improved dialogue. It has been said that foreign businesses know and understand our buying patterns better than we do.

Most non-African American companies are very much aware that African American communities have a disposable income of approximately 300 billion dollars. I stated previously they also are aware that we are more loyal toward price than race. Many companies acknowledge that the margin of profit is determined by the consumption pattern of the African American community. These same companies are very much aware that the African American community not only determines the profit, but often dictates the survival of the company and sometimes the industry.

> African American consumers purchase 18 percent of the orange juice, 20 percent of the rice and Scotch whiskey, 26 percent of the Cadillacs, 31 percent of cosmetics, 35 percent of soft drinks, 38 percent of cigarettes, 39 percent of liquor, and 40 percent of the records and movie tickets. Research indicates that African American consumers are loyal toward "brand name" items. African Americans buy disproportionately more Tide, Uncle Ben's rice, Aunt Jemima products, Kool cigarettes, Quaker grits and oatmeal, Kraft, Southern Comfort, Seagrams, cognac, and many others.[1]

The first step on my economic agenda is to develop more businesses not boycott a company. I do feel that African Americans have the right to expect that their consumption of a company's products will lead to that company to employ some of its members, deposit some of its money in Black banks, advertise in Black media, and make contributions to the African American community. Imagine what would happen to the American economy if the African American consumer decided not to buy any cigarettes, liquor, and soft drinks for a month. Some of these companies treat African American consumers like the Democratic Party treats African American voters. They operate on the assumption that there are no other alternatives for African American consumers, and that our loyalty is so great there is nothing they can do that will be considered disrespectful.

One of the popular arguments that has been used in the discussion of Black economic development is that African American consumers earn $300 billion and spend 93 percent of their money with non-African American businesses. One solution to the unemployment problem is to increase the percentage of purchases made with African American businesses. If African Americans spent only seven percent or about 21 billion, we have the potential to spend 279 billion to put our people back to work. For every billion dollars spent elsewhere, we export 10,000 jobs. I often feel the 300 billion dollar figure seems uncomprehendible. Many people just can not appreciate that mass of money. I also feel that when you mention $300 billion it let's the individual off the hook. I believe we need to break down this large amount so that each individual consumer can assess just what they're doing to contribute to this dilemma.

If the African American consumer has at his/her disposal $1,500 a month, how realistic is it for us to expect that this consumer will be able to spend all of this money with African American businesses? If we looked at a Black business directory you would see some limitations on the variety and magnitude of African American businesses. If the African American consumer in most cities wanted to use $1,500 to go out and buy a 23 inch color television set, compact disc player, VCR, an item at a pet shop, or a part for their gas furnace they may be disappointed when they can't find these items and others in the African American community. This leads us into a discussion of the chicken and the egg theory, whereby maybe the lack of African businesses and diversity is based on the lack of Black consumer support and vice versa. The reality is that African American consumers can not be criticized for not supporting African American businesses for items that African American businesses do not sell. Listed below are ten large categories where most people's incomes are allocated.

1) Food
2) Clothing
3) Housing
4) Utilities
5) Automobile/Transportation
6) Furniture
7) Health & Insurance
8) Entertainment
9) Sundries
10) Contribution

In reviewing these areas individually we need to ask ourselves as a community, how much food can we and do we purchase from African American merchants? In most communities you have marginal corner grocery stores, some owned by African Americans, and then you have a supermarket that buys food not only by the volume, but also owns large farms. The food industry operates under the principles of monopoly capitalism. It makes it very difficult for marginal grocery stores to compete. Parents will often send their children to the corner store for a few items but the bulk of their purchases are made at the large national chain store. I don't know if Black economic development advocates are suggesting that a family of four purchase their entire food budget at the African American corner store, that may not be feasible if the corner store sells a gallon milk for $3.39 and the chain store sells a gallon of milk at $1.69. But recently, under the leadership of Rev. Sampson, the National Black Farmers Harvest, has been actively involved trying to coordinate the Southern Black farmer with the Northern Black consumer. Why should African Americans starve or pay exorbitant prices and the Black farmer is losing his land because he can't find a market? More will be said about this in the last chapter on economic empowerment. Many foreign groceries compete better against the chains because several stores buy together in bulk. Many mom and pop stores could benefit from the African value-Ujamaa (cooperative economics). The main concern is how many African Americans even try to buy their food from African American vendors?

The next area is the clothing industry. How much of our disposable income are we presently spending on clothes and how much realistically can we spend with African American merchants? If African American consumers continue to remain more loyal to Nike, Reebok, L.A. Gear, Louis Vuitton, Bill Blass, and so many others, then African American merchants must stock brand name items at competitive prices. The question then becomes, can an individual African American merchant compete with national chain stores on designer items? An African American consumer wants to buy a pair of "Air Jordans"; the national chain store purchases a million of these shoes-that by the way were made in Asia for eight dollars. The American consumer is charged between $150.00 and $200.00. If the larger retailers, out of the graciousness of their hearts, want to lower their profit margin by selling the eight dollar shoe at $100.00 there remains a good profit margin for the manufacturer, wholesaler, and retailer. It becomes difficult for the independent merchant, who only purchased 200 of those shoes to sell them for less.

Complete the values chart below.

Item	Needs	Wants
Vegetables		
Pork		
Fruit		
Cake/Ice Cream		
Designer Dress		
School Coat		
Designer Coat		
Three Bedroom House		
Two Bedroom Apartment		
Sixteen Room Mansion		
Ford Taurus		
Cadillac		
BMW		
Queen Size Bed		
King Size Bed		
Vacation To Hawaii		
Trip To Family Reunion		
Health Club Membership		
Liquor		
Lottery		
Tithe		

It's a very interesting combination in the clothing industry because on the one hand many African Americans are very "brand" conscious. They are obsessed with designer labels, and yet are also very price conscious. On the Jesse Jackson show, an African American male in the audience commented that he had designed a shoe that he demonstrated on national television which was almost identical to the "pumps" that our youth presently value. When asked how much did the shoe retail for, he answered, "$28.00." The audience laughed because they thought it had to be poor quality because it was too cheap. I often wonder about a people who say they are concerned about price and the lack of funds and then spend $100 plus for a label. It's obvious many are not interested in the liberation of the community.

The next commodity is housing. Consumer interaction exists with the landlord, mortgage company and real estate agent. How much of our budget can we spend with each other in the housing industry? It has been said that land is more important than money because money can be produced in a factory and the United States government has demonstrated that this reduces the value of money. You can not make land in a factory. Governments do not go to war over money. They go to war over land and its natural resources. Sixty to 90 percent of the property in the African American community is owned by non-African Americans. We need to own the property in our neighborhoods. We should strive for African American consumers to rent from African American landlords or buy a house from an African American and both parties represented by African American real estate agents. It is even more ideal when the mortgage can be financed by a Black savings and loan or a bank. This is an area where there is great potential for more of our $300 billion to be spent among each other.

The next comprehensive area is utilities. It includes electricity, gas, and telephone. African Americans can not be faulted because they paid their bills to the only companies authorized that were not owned by African Americans. Transportation becomes our next category of interest. Members of the African American community who do not own a car and use public transportation, can't be criticized for using the only corporation available. The purchase of an automobile stimulates two major consumer transactions, the purchasing of the car and the consumption of gasoline; both industries have manufacturers and retailers. Presently, the African American community does not have a car manufacturer, these purchases would have to be made with General Motors, Ford, Chrysler, Honda, Toyota, Nissan, Volkswagen, and others.

There has been great concern about the disrespect that Japanese leaders have shown toward the African American community. African Americans buy upwards of 25 to 30 percent of their cars from Japanese manufacturers. Japanese manufacturers that have plants in America have not placed them near African American communities. Consequently, the labor force is minuscule in comparison to our percentage of purchases. African Americans should demand more from Japanese dealers or consider a boycott.

While African Americans may not be able to direct their dollars toward a Black manufacturer, they can support African American dealers. All that's required is a desire to identify these dealers and purchase the car. Many African American consumers are only concerned about the car, price, proximity, and don't even explore identifying African American dealers that sell the exact same car. This is another area where there is great potential of a portion of our 300 billion dollars being directed toward African American car dealers. The other component of the automobile industry are the manufacturers and retailers of gasoline i.e., Amoco, Shell, Mobil, and others. Here again, African Americans can not be faulted because presently we don't own an oil refining company. We are in a position though to support African American gasoline dealers.

Furniture and appliances is our next division. Earlier, it was mentioned that if you looked in a Black business directory, you may be hardpressed to find a Black owned company that's selling large television sets, VCR's, compact disc players, dining wear, stoves, refrigerators etc. These are large ticket items and they take an immense amount of our 300 billion dollars. Most of these items are purchased through large companies such as Sears, Kmart, JC Penny, Highland, Service Merchandise, and others. Later in the chapter. we're going to talk about buying wholesale because if we must buy from non-African companies we can at least form buying clubs to purchase in bulk, since that is the strategy that these large companies use to make it difficult for African American merchants to compete.

Before we purchase, we should always ask ourselves:
1) Can I make it?
2) Can I barter for it?
3) Can I buy it wholesale?
4) Can I buy it retail from an African American merchant?

The next area is entertainment. This industry encompasses movies, live theater, the record industry, amusement parks, concerts, health clubs, sports, and vacation/travel. In the movie industry, we buy approximately 40 percent of the tickets and only own one moderate size studio which is controlled by Oprah Winfrey. There are no African American distributors, and the Baldwin in Los Angeles remains the only theater showing first run movies. This is what has made it very difficult for independent filmmakers to grow, develop, and thrive. My company made "Up Against the Wall," starring Marla Gibbs. During the production of the movie, I got an opportunity to observe monopoly capitalism, where larger studios own theater chains. Obviously, a movie made by the studios is guaranteed promotion and theatrical space. Paramount owns the Arsenio Hall show and numerous theaters which guarantees promotion and distribution. Many Black theaters can't even secure first run movies. It has been said that during a recession you can always depend on the Black consumer especially in the entertainment industry. I guess because of our oppression, we escape through movies, music, liquor, and drugs. Can you imagine the effect on the industry if we did not buy any movie tickets or records for a month? Can you imagine the record industry without African American musicians and singers? This is another glaring situation where we buy close to 40 percent of the records, contribute the talent to the industry and receive very little financially. Many of our progressive rappers have become concerned with how little they make in stark contrast to the recording companies, distributors, and retailers. Recording companies can play artists against each other until they all say "no deal."

Another component of the entertainment industry is sports. African Americans constitute 86 percent of the NBA basketball starters, 50 percent of the NFL starters, and over 33 percent of the major league baseball starters. In the last chapter, we are going to talk about economic empowerment and two major contributions that African

Americans bring to the table are athletes and entertainers. We have made tremendous accomplishments in sports and music. We control very little of the industry, however, it would be drastically affected and may not be able to survive without our contribution. Can you imagine the NBA without African American ballplayers? The Negro Baseball League was thriving, playing before large crowds. The integration of Major League Baseball created the demise of the Negro Baseball League. We lost Black baseball teams that were businesses and the ancillary businesses that go along with running a franchise. Today, many sport teams play in the suburbs, ticket prices are exorbitant and purchased in advance by corporate America making it prohibitive for the average family to see a game. The tremendous demand by the White community to see Michael Jordan fly through the air has created so many season ticket holders that even members of the African American community that have the funds find it difficult to secure tickets. Many inner city children in Chicago have never seen Michael Jordan play. I commend Dave Winfield for buying tickets for inner city children. The large amusement parks such as Great America, Six Flags, Disney World, Disney Land, and so many others are not owned by African Americans. We can not be blamed for dispensing part of our monies in an area where there are few African American alternatives. When African Americans choose to go on a vacation and desire to fly, there are no African American airlines they can support. There was one in Atlanta called Air Atlanta, but it no longer exists. This also applies to lodging; most hotels are not owned by African Americans. There has been a positive suggestion made by Tony Brown, Walter Fauntroy, and others over the years that we'll discuss in detail in the last chapter on economic empowerment. It entails the collection of funds that will be used for the building of four regional hotels that will accommodate the large numbers of African Americans that travel for vacations and conferences. In the meantime, we can utilize African American travel agents.

The last two areas of the entertainment industry that I want to discuss are concerts and live theater. There is a need for the African American community to benefit more from a sold out Michael Jackson, Janet Jackson, M.C. Hammer, Prince, Anita Baker, and Whitney Houston concert. We are not receiving a great return on our investment when many of these concert halls hold 10 to

20 thousand people averaging 30 to 40 dollars per ticket and the only African Americans that are receiving any of the funds are those you see on stage. African American entertainers have to demand more from concert promoters and consider performing in smaller houses that are owned by African Americans. In most large urban areas there are several Black theater organizations. There is a need for the African American consumer to support live theater.

Health and Insurance is the next classification. I would like to believe that there remain only a few African Americans that believe that White doctors and dentists are more qualified than African American doctors and dentists. One of the major hurdles in this industry is that we are approximately 12 to 15 percent of the population, depending upon which statistics you're reviewing, but less than two percent of the doctors and dentists. African American consumers need more African American doctors and hospitals. We must maintain Meharry Medical School. There are many rural areas of the south where there are few, if any, African American doctors, and the only one available would require a one to two hour drive from a metropolitan area. In many cities, we have lost our only Black hospital because of the lack of support from Black consumers and doctors. African American consumers face a dilemma when their doctor has a residency at a White hospital and the African American consumer would like to support an African American hospital. African American doctors are in a difficult position if they have residency at an African American hospital and the African American consumer prefers not to be treated in that institution.

There are presently 30 Black insurance companies nationwide, with North Carolina Mutual, mentioned in the chapter on the history of Black economics being the leader. The insurance industry is going through a great degree of havoc because of the large numbers of medical claims and the cost of hospitalization. Most companies, Black and White are losing money. Consumers are expecting a greater return on their investment from insurance companies, creating a tighter profit margin for all companies. It remains difficult for most of these companies to compete against Allstate, Blue Cross and Blue Shield, State Farm, Prudential, New York Life and others. I do believe this is an industry that African American consumers can support their businesses can improve. In most cities African American consumers simply are not aware that these companies exist and there is a need for African American insurance companies to become more visible through advertising.

The next to last area is sundries. This category represents all of the miscellaneous items i.e., novelties, drugs, and other services. The largest number of African American businesses probably fall in this category i.e., barbers, beauticians, shoe repairs, cleaners, and retail stores. If we take a look at our $1,500 monthly check we may spend $100 to $200 in this category. African Americans have great potential to empower themselves in this arena.

The final item is contributions, primarily to churches, civil rights organizations, colleges, and other worthwhile causes. Unfortunately, the majority of Black churches have their monies deposited in White banks. Black colleges receive 16 percent of the students, but produce over 37 percent of the graduates. Unfortunately, there are large numbers of alumni of Black colleges that do not feel the need to contribute to the institution that gave them a solid educational foundation. The larger African American community should not be dependent on Bill Cosby and Oprah Winfrey to finance African American students. Most institutions have found the most effective way to secure contributions is not through chicken dinners, raffle tickets, bake sales, bingo, and entertainment activities, but through regular payroll deductions. The United Way has been very successful at aligning itself with corporate America and other large public institutions by using these deductions. Their slogan, "It Works for All of Us," may not be totally true. They receive a much greater percentage of deductions from African Americans in comparison to the amount of money they contribute to African American organizations. A review of the larger recipients of United Way contributions leads us to the Red Cross and medical organizations. The largest African American recipient is the Urban League.

There is a group that has been doing a tremendous amount of work in the African American community since the mid '60s, The Black United Fund. The Fund has also structured itself to receive payroll deductions. Unfortunately, The United Way has made it arduous for them to be more effective. African American employees should express to their corporations that they would like to have an option on where their contributions are directed; and would prefer The Black United Fund. The history of The Black United Fund is that they support Black organizations involved in a myriad of activities including housing for low income residents.

The desire in this chapter is to develop a more economically literate consumer who is also loyal to supporting African American businesses. The next area that we need to look at is the development of a budget. Most people are not cognizant where there $1,500 actually is spent. The budget then becomes the blueprint for how we build a nation. We also need to make some distinctions between needs and wants. There is a rumor that African Americans buy what they want and beg for what they need.

It is also important for the African American consumer to understand that stores are designed such that when you're closer to the cashier more effort is placed into enticing the consumer to make a spontaneous purchase. Advertising is more effective, the design of the floor space is more creative, and items are lower in price. When you near the check-out counter, items are priced between 25 cents and $3 with the hope that an item of this value will not require much of a decision. Many consumers are not aware that 60 percent of their purchases are made on impulse. Consumers must acknowledge that it is suicidal to go into a store without a list. They must also have the discipline to stick to it.

It is especially important for African American males to develop a budget, because many keep their monies in their pockets as sort of a ego boost and could not explain at the end of a day or a week where "the wad" of money in their pocket was dispersed. An effective technique for consumers would be buying out of season. Many retailers will lower the prices of various items when those items are not in demand. For example, snow blowers are going to be more expensive during a snow storm than in the month of July. Swim wear will be cheaper in December than in July. The season of Kwanzaa was established to represent the harvest which represents the end of the year and in America that will represent the last week of the calendar year. Kwanzaa is also in a position to take advantage of "after Christmas sales." Effective shoppers know this week is a very good time to purchase. Out of season shopping should be coupled with increased utilization of coupons. It is unfortunate that the people with the least income use coupons less than those more financially stable. This also applies to prices where those on welfare and others less affluent pay higher prices than others with larger salaries. It is very frustrating to witness slightly yellow bananas selling for 25 cents a pound in an affluent suburb, and in a low income inner city neighborhood over ripe bananas selling for 69 cents a pound.

Another book could be written on the impact that welfare has had on our people and how it is used by the government to break the spirits of our people. The United States government has chosen to pay $500.00 a month in AFDC and food stamps times 12 months which equals $6,000 times 40 years totaling $240,000 dollars rather than to educate someone who will earn $20,000 per year times 40 years for a total income of $800,000, of which they will receive approximately 25 percent or $200,000 in taxes. The $240,000 they paid to welfare recipients and the $200,000 they lost when they did not educate that person would have been beneficial to both the government and the tax payer. The government is willing to break the spirits of people because oppression means more than economics.

Looking at the African American consumer and reviewing our disposable income, 25 percent of our race makes over $40,000. One-third of our race lives below the poverty line. There is a widening gap between the Black "haves" and the "have nots." Three distinct income groups exist in the African American community. There is a growing middle class, a working poor fighting very hard to make ends meet, and a group some call "the underclass." I often marvel when people talk about the Black community because they talk about it as if it's monolithic; in actuality, there are distinguishable income levels. Unfortunately, some of our people identify more with income and class than with race. The origins of this in America are in slavery with the "house negro" and the "field negro." African Americans are approximately 14 percent of the population and only earn seven percent of the total income. We own less than three percent of the wealth in America. In 1940 the median income of African Americans was only 40 percent of that of Whites. In 1970, it was 61 percent. In 1989 it dropped down to 57 percent. This is a loss of income of $1.7 trillion.

White liberals often think that this gap in median income is because of education. A Black male with a college degree earns $26,550. A White male with a college degree earns $35,701. This is a 26 percent difference. A Black male with a graduate degree will earn $35,850 and a White male with the same degree will earn $42,063. This is a 15 percent difference. African American females only earn 84 percent of what Black males earn, which of course is less than what White males earn. Whites with amnesia and Blacks who do not know their history advocate that racism is not the culprit, but the lack of a strong work ethic is to blame. It is obvious that they are not aware of this research or the latest reports of discrimination by employment agencies. Racism is real and it does not motivate African Americans to strive for excellence when they're not paid according to their qualifications.

In the meantime, African Americans can not allow racism to stifle their desire to grow and develop. Dempsey Travis reminds us in his book *Racism: America's Corporate Gift,* that we should be politically astute to recognize we are not in "our" corporations and different rules apply, understanding racism will reduce surprises, frustrations, depression, and suicides.[2]

Beyond racism, African American consumers need to ask themselves what do they do with the money they receive? I believe the acid test on who owns your life, lies in your answer to the question, could you quit your job tomorrow? Many people who think they are members of the middle class would find, if they miss one paycheck, they would no longer be a part of the Black middle class, but part of the working or underclass. I don't believe you can be in a "class" off one paycheck. There is a distinction between income and wealth. Income requires that you continue to work either for someone or yourself. Wealth is the accumulation of assets that create income for you.

Time is wealth. People who spend their entire lives working will not have any time to enjoy it. If a person does not like what they do and spends 50 weeks of a year doing it, they will only have two weeks to enjoy themselves. If we look at what American consumers have done from the time they began working until the age of 65, 29 people out of a 100 people died, 63 people are financially dependent, four are financially stable, three have to work, and only one of them is wealthy.[3]

This is a sad commentary for people that worked 40 years. Listed is a table illustrating monthly income and total income over a 40 year period.

If we worked 40 years and earned a monthly salary of $2,000, we would have earned approximately $1,000,000. However, if not properly invested, and unaware of effective consumer strategies only one out of a 100 will be wealthy. Many African Americans are dependent on Social Security, which was never designed to be a complete source of retirement income, but as a supplement to additional wealth generated throughout a person's working career. At the inception of Social Security in the mid 1930s, there were over 30 workers for every one recipient. Presently, there are seven workers per one recipient, by the year 2000 and beyond it's estimated there will be three workers per every one recipient.

There are many reasons why only one out of a 100 Americans becomes wealthy and only four are financially stable. Those reasons include lack of goals, lack of information, procrastination, and attitude. Many people do not have a budget. They could not tell you where the $1500 or $2000 was spent this month much less explain where $960,000 went over their 40 year careers. The first step in addressing the problem of lack of goals is to ask yourself, what is my plan? when do I want to retire? what will the cost of living be? how much will I need? and how will I achieve this goal?

A person who says they want to retire in 20 years should consume less during that period. If a person says that they want to live on an income very close to their present income then that means their investment portfolio should reflect an aggressive desire to create income for that period. If a person says they don't want to retire for another thirty years then they may be in a position to delay investment for a few years. If a person says that they want to be dependent on their children when their 65, they shouldn't worry about shopping without a list and keeping their savings in a shoe box.

The second major problem is the lack of information. Most African Americans are not aware of the differences in investment strategies and insurance, and the impact of taxes and inflation on overall wealth. Most African Americans did not grow up in households where members possessed investment instruments. The third reason for the lack of wealth is procrastination. Most

Wealth = Money x Yield x Time

Monthly Income	Ten Years	Twenty Years	Thirty Years	Forty Years
$500	$60,000	$120,000	$180,000	$240,000
$600	$72,000	$144,000	$216,000	$288,000
$800	$96,000	$192,000	$288,000	$384,000
$1,000	$120,000	$240,000	$360,000	$480,000
$1,500	$180,000	$360,000	$540,000	$720,000
$2,000	$240,000	$480,000	$720,000	$960,000
$2,500	$300,000	$600,000	$900,000	$1,200,000
$3,000	$360,000	$720,000	$1,084,000	$1,440,000

people have been made aware of certain strategies that can be used to generate wealth, but choose not to make a decision--no decision is a decision not to grow and develop.

Another reason is attitude and there are numerous components that contribute to a negative attitude toward economic development and wealth. Les Brown, George Subira, and Venita Van Caspel have done an excellent job of reviewing some of the attitudinal barriers that prevent people from maximizing their investments. One component of attitude that hinders wealth is not being able to think "big." Many people simply can not comprehend a million dollars; they're satisfied "just making it" and that term reflects what they think of themselves. Many of us create our own limitation.

Another reason is that we grew up in a church that taught us money was a source of evil and a true Christian suffers on earth and receives their reward in heaven. Many people actually believe that a good Christian could not be a millionaire. Every good and perfect gift comes from God and money is not the source of all evil--what matters is how people use it. Thank God Bill Cosby chose to give 20 million dollars to Spelman College rather than building more B1 Bombers. Some people involved in the Black liberation struggle also correlate commitment with poverty. Those who are committed surely could not be the one out of a 100 that was wealthy or one of the four persons that were financially stable because they were in the "struggle." I postulate the word struggle turns

Listed below is a chart that I want you to complete describing a typical month's expenditures.

Food	Budgeted Amount	Black Business	Non-Black Business
Clothing			
Housing			
Utilities			
Transportaion			
Furniture			
Health & Insurance			
Entertainment			
Sundries			
Contributions			

people off. No one wants to struggle indefinitely. Is it wrong for someone involved in the liberation of their people to want medical insurance, safe housing, and a college education for their children?

Additional hindrance has been our desire for a guarantee, whether it's a job or an investment. Many African Americans are looking for a guarantee. They would prefer a guaranteed salary than a percentage of an unlimited amount of income. They would rather receive a lower guaranteed fixed rate of return than to potentially receive a higher rate of return without the guarantee. Very few people grown rich with all of their monies invested in a guaranteed source of income.

Lastly, most people go their entire lives and never find something that captures their interest to the extent that they'll spend almost every waking moment strategizing about it. People that are intense are able to channel a very large majority if not all of their energies into one endeavor until it is successful completion. People that are self-actualized seldom, if at all use the word "can't." Many people are defeated in the pursuit of their dream from the very beginning because they have convinced themselves that it "can't" be achieved. My request is that we remove the word from our vocabulary.

Before we explore how to develop income into wealth we need to understand there are only three things that can be done with money. It can be spent, invested, or remain idle. Earlier in this chapter, we talked about a better way to spend our money. It needs to be spent as much as possible with African American businesses and we need to make distinctions between 'needs' and 'wants.' All this should be based upon a budget.

> Very little money remains idle or invested in the American economy. Americans save less than anybody else and African Americans save less than White Americans. Americans save 4.8 percent of their income compared to 14.4 percent for West Germans, 15.5 percent by the French and 20 percent by the Japanese.[4]

I define money that is idle as money that's in a checking account or in your house not earning any interest.

I would like to spend this portion of the chapter looking at investment strategies. We have to begin to think like our ancestors who built pyramids for the next generations. We can't build programs designed only to last two and three years when our ancestors built pyramids that have lasted for over four thousand years. We have to begin to look at transferring wealth over to our children.

An excellent example of a family transferring wealth to their children is the Evans family featured in the October 1990 issue of Black Enterprise. Twelve family members have invested $800.00 a month for five years and now have accumulated $2.3 million. They have outperformed the Dow Jones Industrial average by a margin of three to one, one yielding an impressive 30 percent annual return.

This family understood that assets that are worn on your back or those that you drive in depreciate in value very quickly. I've noticed in the African American community, because of our low levels of self-esteem many of us feel that we have to impress people by wearing our entire salary on our back or driving in it. I've also observed more luxury cars in low-income areas than in affluent suburbs. Many people do not possess self-esteem but " material " esteem. Their self-worth is predicated on their possessions. If they are not driving in their Cadillac or wearing designer clothes then their self-esteem is greatly reduced. Earlier, I indicated that time is wealth and many people have become slaves to their cars and clothes. As a result, they are unable to retire or quit their jobs and start their own businesses because their possessions have them deep in debt.

I would much rather drive a regular car, be able to start my own business, and retire when I want to than to drive a Mercedes (causing a great degree of mercy) that forces me to work longer for someone else. I've observed business owners, who in their attempt to convince the community of their success have taken monies out of the business that should have been used for additional investments. These same business owners have used that money to purchase a luxury car and other extravagant possessions. It is not that I am against people having the finer things in life, but I do believe that people who earn $300 billion a year should be able to generate more than $3,200 per person in wealth.

There are 10,000 people in America who become millionaires annually. That's one per 1,075 persons. There are several ways to become wealthy in America, inheritance, investment, real estate, salaries and royalties, owning your own business, and the lottery. Forbes magazine has documented that of the 200,000 + millionaires in America, 38 percent of them receive their wealth through inheritance.[5]

These people are the offspring of their ancestors who took advantage of the Homestead Act, Land Redemption Act, slavery, and good old fashioned "Old Money." It doesn't take much skill to be a millionaire off the backs of our ancestors who were not paid for their labor.

Thirty-eight percent of these millionaires also earn their wealth through owning their businesses. This is a very important area for African Americans to consider because 98 percent of the African American population that earns over $50,000.00 receive its income through businesses not salaries.[6]

African Americans who own their businesses have five times the net worth of those who earn their incomes through salaries.[7]

Unfortunately, over 50 percent of college educated African Americans work for the government.[8]

This "good job" is not the best way to create wealth. Nineteen percent of the wealthiest people in America produce their wealth through real estate, four percent receive their income through the investment of stocks and bonds, and less than one percent through salaries, royalties, and the lottery. Since very few African Americans are going to inherit a million dollars, we should concentrate our efforts on business ownership, real estate, and investments in stocks and bonds. The objective of building personal wealth can only be achieved with a set of priorities, goals, and values. I personally believe that it is important that those areas you value most should be paid first. The phrase African Americans buy what "they want" and beg for what they "need" is not the kind of priority I'm recommending in building personal wealth. My value system dictates that we should pay God first. That one statement could generate another book. There are adults who grew up in the church and as a child gave a quarter, gave a dollar as a teenager, and as an adult now give five dollars. Many of these adults make $20,000.00 or more but have a five dollar mentality as it relates to contributing to the church. There are numerous reasons for this rationale. Many people feel that their money belongs to them and not God. They feel they earned the money not God. Others believe more money goes to the pastor than to community programs. There are others who say they love the Lord but don't need the church and can avoid contributions. Others feel their salaries are too large for 10 percent to remain applicable.

The Bible is clear on giving God back 10 percent of what you earn. The laws of prosperity reinforce that, because your gift will be multiplied as it returns back to you. I don't disagree with the prosperity rationale but I don't give to God and the church because I'm looking for a three to one return. I simply feel thankful that I've been able to earn this standard of living and to whom much is given, much is required. I thank God for allowing me to have the other 90 percent, because it all came from Him.

I believe the second step in the plan after giving God His is to pay yourself second - pay God first and pay yourself second. Savings is the way you pay yourself. Unfortunately, most people save whatever is left after their expenditures rather than savings being an itemized deduction that is paid at the beginning. Americans, as mentioned earlier save less than most countries in the industrialized world.

Americans save an average of 4.8 percent of their income. African Americans that have savings accounts have an average balance of $2,100. Whites have an average balance is $4,000. Approximately 34 percent of African American adults have a checking account versus 79 percent in the White community.[9]

One of the most effective ways to ensure savings is the automatic deduction either from the payroll check or the checking account. Most people do not have the discipline to formally write a check toward savings on a monthly basis. Consequently, the payroll deduction or the deduction through the checking account is a very effective way to ensure that savings will take place on an ongoing regular basis. African Americans have their savings in a wide range of areas. They include a sock, shoe box, can, checking account, passbook account, certificate of deposit, money market, mutual funds, stocks and bonds, IRA's, Self-Employment Pension Plans, annuities, and real estate. It should be obvious to all that there will be very little interest earned if your money is tied up in a sock, shoe box or a can. Remember, there was a time when African Americans were not allowed to invest in White financial instruments.

On the average passbook accounts pay four to five percent and certificates of deposits pay six to eight percent. Money markets pays six to nine percent interest and mutual funds pay between seven and 15 percent. Stocks, bonds, and real estate have an unlimited percentage of interest. Pension Plans and IRA's can be invested in any number of the above areas. The criteria for which area to invest savings should be based on liquidity, rate of return, inflation, taxes, and a guarantee. Placing money in a sock, shoe box, can, or checking account satisfies liquidity and it does not increase tax liability. It does not generate a rate of return, nor does it keep up with inflation. The first three are as safe as any other possessions in your house and they run the risk of being stolen. A checking account, passbook account, and certificate of deposit are all insured by federal agencies at the level of $100,000 per account. Investing the money in a pass- book account will also keep the money liquidable. The rate of return will be small and will not keep up with inflation. It also does not create a significant tax liability. Investing monies in certificates of deposit garners a greater interest rate, but you do lose liquidity because of the one to four year requirements without penalty and loss of interest. This investment, creating an interest rate of six to seven percent will be commensurate to the present level of inflation and it will create marginal tax liability. The money market account is very similar to the certificate of deposit in terms of rate of return, tax liability, and inflation, but it does allow for greater liquidity and a slightly higher interest rate. Many African Americans have their monies in these first areas because a guarantee is very important to them.

The people who have been able to create the greatest wealth though have their monies primarily in the areas of money markets, mutual funds, stocks, bonds, pensions, and real estate. Most of these investments do not come with a guarantee nor do they offer as much liquidity. But if you think about a bank or a savings and loan that is offering you four percent in a passbook account and six percent in a certificate of deposit, it should provoke you to realize that the bank has to be earning an interest rate higher than the above in order to stay in business. The question then becomes, where are banks earning 10, 15 and 20 percent to pay consumers four to six percent? The answer lies in mutual funds, stocks, bonds, and real estate. While they have no guarantee that these investments are secure, they are very confident that when those instruments fail so will checking accounts, passbook accounts, and certificates of deposit. The interrelationship between these two sources is direct. The investments in mutual funds, stocks and bonds, and real estate are advantageous in offering a greater rate of return, a hedge against inflation, and also create greater tax liability unless the investment is a tax exempt instrument. It becomes very important that African Americans understand the relationship between the rate of return and tax liability. If an African American is in the 33 percent tax bracket and has an option of investing $10,000.00 in mutual funds at a 12 percent return, or in a tax free annuity at 10 percent, it makes greater tax sense to invest in the annuity. The annual interest on the mutual funds was $1,200.00 while the annuity only paid $1,000.00, but the taxes were $400.00 on the mutual funds leaving a net return of $800.00 in comparison to the full $1,000.00 tax free income via the annuity. Investments in pension plans are very advantageous because none of the investment creates a tax liability while they're generating income, and are only taxable when monies are deducted during the retirement stage.

It is amazing how African Americans shy away from investments that create a greater rate of return, because those investments are not insured, or guaranteed, but a large number will give money to the Lottery. Many African Americans tell me that they do not have any money to save and yet they spend more than $50 a month on the Lottery. Twelve dollars and fifty cents per week may not seem significant, but $50 a month invested in money market, mutual funds, stocks, and bonds at a 12 percent interest rate will create a much greater return than the remote possibility of winning the Lottery.

I believe it would be more advantageous for African Americans to invest fifty dollars a month in a mutual fund than in the Lottery. Investing $50 a month or $600 a year at a 12 percent interest rate will turn into $96,838 in 20 years, in 30 years it will become $324,351, and in 40 years it will blossom into $1,030,970. Unfortunately, the people who are short term oriented do not envision a future and do not think about transferring wealth to their children and would rather play an instant rich scheme called the Lottery, where the chances of success are remote at best, than to invest in an instrument with a proven track record of success and receive over a million dollars in 40 years off a $50 dollar a month investment.

There are many reasons for our failure to take advantage of these investment instruments. Historically, we were denied the right to invest. Most African American families do not have members who have invested in money markets, mutual funds, stocks and bonds, and real estate. Another reason is the lack of advertising. Most of these instruments do not aggressively advertise and especially in the African American community. If you look in any newspaper or listen to the electronic media you will be exposed more to advertising promoting the Lottery than you will be to mutual funds, stocks, bonds, and real estate. There is also the assumption that to invest in money markets, mutual funds, stocks, and bonds requires a large sum of money versus the one to five dollar ticket playing the lottery. Money market, mutual funds, stocks, and bonds can be secured for less than $100. Mutual funds can be purchased for as low as $30.

There is a law called Rule 72 (72 divided by interest equals the number of years to double investment) which most people have never been taught. It's also unfortunate that in America you can receive an elementary, high school and college education and never be taught Rule 72. If you earn 1 percent on your money, it will take 72 years for $1.00 to become $2.00. Listed below is a graphic design of Rule 72.[10]

RULE 72

1% = 72 years	At a 12 percent return,
4% = 18 years	$10,000.00 becomes:
5% = 14.4 years	$20,000.00 in 6 years
6% = 12 years	$40,000.00 in 12 years
10% = 7.2 years	$80,000.00 in 18 years
12% = 6 years	$160,000.00 in 24 years
18% = 4 years	$320,000.00 in 30 years
24% = 3 years	$640,000.00 in 36 years

If African Americans have the ability to read the sports pages and figure out all of the procedures related to horse racing then they have the ability to read the stock pages. For many African Americans, money is not liquid because it's tied up in clothes, cars, and houses. I often ask my audiences, If your mother were in jail today and bond was set at $50,000, and you needed 10 percent to secure her release, would you be able to respond? I was very disappointed in the production of our movie, "Up Against the Wall," when I solicited from the African American community $5,000 investments with a 15 percent rate of return guaranteed by our mutual funds to be repaid in six months and African Americans who were in a position to respond to that request. Many African Americans simply are unable to take advantage of very good investment opportunities or respond to crises that could arise because of how monies are allocated.

I mentioned earlier that 19 percent of the wealthiest people in the world derived their income through real estate. Land is the only asset that can not be reproduced. Countries go to war over land. If we surveyed the neighborhoods in which we live and researched how much of the land and the buildings in our community are actually owned by African Americans, we would be gravely disappointed. It becomes imperative that African Americans begin to own the land and buildings in which they live. We can not allow foreigners to continue to be prosperous absentee landlords. African Americans who have been successful in real estate have certain characteristics and traits. One is that they have a large vision. One of the major problems in our community is that for many of our people we think very small. We think of lottery tickets and gambling strategies that may generate a $100, but very few of our people think about a $100,000 to a million dollar project. Real Estate allows that kind of opportunity. Secondly, these people have developed an adequate and substantial net worth creating the kind of collateral and leverage positions needed to negotiate with banks. Thirdly, they understand the concept of OPM (other people's money). They understand that in real estate one of the most effective things to do is to use opm for investment. Astute investors in real estate try to place the least down payment on property and spread the payments over a long period of time.

Remember, one of the most effective strategies in personal finances is to understand the concept of inflation. This concept is to repay today's debt with money that will be of less value in the future. For example, if a piece of property is available for $100,000, a wise person in real estate would try very hard to secure the property for 10 percent or less down payment. Obviously, a person who does not have $5,000 to $10,000 may be unsuccessful in securing the property. Another alternative for the person who does not have this much money in liquid assets is to have it in long term assets and use it as collateral when negotiating with a bank. Many investors have found properties that were in foreclosure and were able to secure them very inexpensively. They then refurbished and sold the property in 60 or 90 days for a substantial profit. This effort only requires the ability to identify properties in foreclosure, identify quality, price competitive contractors, and have an aggressive sales strategy. Real Estate is an excellent investment because it is a hedge against inflation, there are depreciation expenses that can be written off to reduce tax liability, it increases equity, and it brings an excellent rate of return. Self-starters could create a great degree of wealth if they simply had five to $10,000 available for investment, ample net worth for leverage, and if they had access to a responsible contractor.

On a more personal note, it behooves all home owners to request from their bank, the amortization schedule. This is a schedule that explains how your mortgage payment is allocated over the areas of principal and interest. Most people are not aware that their $60,000 mortgage over 30 years will actually cost them $180,000. Most people are also not aware that accelerating the principal payments would allow them to reduce the total cost of the mortgage up to 50 percent. Listed below is an example of an amortization schedule for one calendar year. It shows the date, principal, and interest of a monthly mortgage of $573.80 on a $60,000.00 house.

Date	Principal	Interest
January	$102.46	$471.34
February	$103.39	$470.41
March	$104.34	$469.46
April	$105.30	$468.50
May	$106.26	$467.54
June	$107.23	$466.57
July	$108.22	$465.58
August	$109.21	$464.59
September	$110.21	$463.59
October	$111.22	$462.58
November	$112.24	$461.56
December	$113.26	$460.54

The concept of accelerating the principal payment means that in the month of January when you pay the full mortgage of principal and interest you can also pay just the portion of principal for the month of February. As a result, you do not have to pay the interest for the month of February. When you make your payment for February you will now be paying the principal and interest for March. If a person continued in this mode over the course of 12 months they would have eliminated interest payments for six months. In this one year based on the above amortization schedule they would have saved $2,793 in interest.

This strategy is significant in terms of monies that you actually save, but it also has disadvantages that need to be shared with an accountant or tax preparer. The disadvantages of accelerating mortgage payments are tax liability and inflation. You would think that there would be nothing wrong with saving $90,000 and paying the mortgage in 15 rather than 30 years. One factor that needs to be considered before this is pursued is tax liability. A person concerned about taxes, and everyone should be, is always looking for tax write-offs and real estate is excellent, the interest, insurance, and property taxes can be written off. If a person accelerated his/her mortgage payments and were able to pay the full mortgage in 15 years versus 30, it leaves them with 15 years of not having a significant tax write-off at years' end. It would then become important for this person to place this mortgage payment in an investment instrument that will be able to pay for the additional tax liability.

The second reason why some people object to saving $90,000 is because of inflation where they have used present dollars to repay a long-term debt which does not make good inflationary sense. The assumption is that money in the future will be of less value than money in the present. Therefore, you should not use present dollars to repay a long-term futuristic debt. I think all factors need to be considered, but I'd lean toward saving $90,000 and investing in some additional instruments. It's also important that we understand that the Social Security system was not designed to be a full source of income and under its present structure there will be less workers per recipient in the future. In its earlier years, there were 30 or more workers per recipient. Presently it's a five to one ratio and by the year 2000 it will be three to one. Legislation should be passed that African American males be exempt from paying Social Security until the life expectancy exceeds 65.

Most astute people have created additional retirement plans beyond Social Security. They include IRA's, self-employment plans, and annuities. The first three plans allow a write-off of $2,000 per person and some up to 15 percent of your total income to be placed in investment instruments with no tax liability both in the initial investment and throughout the life of the plan. What this means is a person making $20,000 a year could allocate $2,000 a year in an IRA and receive an immediate tax deduction. Secondly, the interest off the $2,000 being placed in a mutual fund or other money bearing instrument would also not be taxed. Tax Liability would not begin until a deduction or withdrawal was made and that would not be until the age of 59, unless a person chose to do it prematurely and received a penalty and a reduction of interest. This kind of retirement planning is advantageous as it relates to tax liability, rate of return, and a hedge against inflation. Unfortunately, the African American community is not taking advantage of this kind of investment strategy at the magnitude of other groups. I believe the reason for this is not because income is not available, but because of short-term values and lack of exposure.

There is a great degree of confusion in the African American community concerning insurance. Our community is under siege from agents who do not always have the best interest of our people in mind when they make their sales presentations. I believe the analogy between African American parents looking to African American public educators for direction is parallel to African American consumers looking to African American insurance agents and financial planners for direction as it relates to the proper insurance to purchase. Many of these insurance agents do a much better job of representing their company and selling products that are available regardless of whether it's in the best financial interest of the community. In very succinct terms Life Insurance is for dying. Investments are for living. The two should never be combined. Life insurance is only needed until you have created an estate large enough where the life insurance can be cancelled. There is no need to continue to pay premiums on a Life Insurance policy when there are no dependents and

HOW TO READ A MUTUAL FUND COLUMN IN THE NEWSPAPER

1. The first column is the fund's abbreviated name. Several funds listed under a single heading indicate a family of funds.

2. The second column in the Net Assets Value (NAV) share at the close of the preceding business day. In some newspapers, the (NAV) is identified as the sell or the bid price — the amount (per share) you would receive if you sold your shares (less any deferred sales charges). Each mutual fund determines its net asset value of its shares outstanding. On any given day, you can determine the value of your holdings by multiplying the NAV by the number of shares you own.

3. The third column is the offering price, or, in some papers, the buy or the asked price. This is the price you would pay if you purchased shares. The buy price is the NAV plus sales charges. If there are no sales charges, an NL for no-load appears in this column, and buy price is the same as the NAV. To figure the sales charge percentage, divide the difference between the NAV and the offering price by the offering price. Here, for instance, the sales charge is 8.5 percent ($13.83 less $12.65 = $1.61 divided by $13.83 = 0.085).

4. The fourth column shows the change, if any, in net assets value from the preceding quotation, in other words, the change over the most recent one-day trading period. This fund, for example, gained ten cents per share.

MUTUAL FUND QUOTATIONS

ABT Midwest Funds:			
Emrg Gr	9.84	10.75+	.12
Growth I	13.95	15.25+	.02
Int Govt	10.61	N.L.+	.01
LG Govt	10.60	11.04	
Sec Inc	11.26	12.31+	.02
Util Inc	14.72	16.09+	.07
Acorn Fnd	42.41	N.L.+	.25
Adtek Fd	12.66	N.L.+	.12
Advest Advantage:			
Govt	9.92	N.L.+	.02
Growth	11.00	N.L.+	.02
Income	10.42	N.L.+	.02
Spacl	10.34	N.L.+	.07
Atuture Fd	15.24	N.L.+	.12
AIM Funds:			
Charter	8.30	N.L.+	.07
Constel	29.54	N.L.+	.20
Conv Yld	13.41	14.34+	.06
Grnwav	10.98	11.74+	.10
American Capital Group:			
Comstk	16.43	17.96+	.10
Corp Bd	7.60	8.31	
Enterpr	15.44	16.87+	.28
Exch Fd	58.52	(z)+	.07
Fd Amer	12.65	13.83+	.09
Govt Sec	11.77	12.62	
Growth	27.28	(z)+	.13
Harbor	15.72	16.67+	.10
High Yld	10.90	11.69	
Muni Bd	20.54	22.20+	.02
Pace Fd	12.19	13.32+	.18
Prov Inc	5.12	5.52+	.02
TxE HY	12.16	12.77	
Venture	17.31	18.92+	.09

Spl Incm	(z)	(z)	.01
Tax ExB	12.36	N.L.+	.01
Third Cn	8.10	N.L.+	.02
Eagle Gth	8.16	8.92–	.02
Eaton Vance Funds:			
Cal Mn r	10.12	N.L.+	.02
EH Stk	14.68	15.83+	.08
Gov Obli	12.47	13.32–	.96
Growth	8.22	8.98+	.09
Hi Mun r	10.18	N.L.+	.02
High Yld	5.26	5.64+	.01
Inc Bost	10.30	11.05+	.02
Invests	8.48	9.27+	.03
Muni Bd	14.00	15.30+	.04
Naut Fd	8.80	9.14+	.01
Spc Eqtv	21.84	23.55+	.20
Tax Mge	21.49	23.49+	.14
VS Specl	14.02	15.22+	.11
Empir Bld	16.62	17.45+	.08
ES Tot rt	14.01	N.L.+	.08
Evergrn	14.55	N.L.+	.07
Evgrgn TR	19.23	N.L.+	.07
Fairmnt	234.95	N.L.+	2.95
Farm B Gr	(z)	(z)	
Federated Group:			
Fed StkB	15.72	N.L.+	.07
Cash Tr	11.10	N.L.+	.01
Exch Fd	50.61	N.L.+	.27
FT Intl	19.75	N.L.+	.04
GISI	9.75	10.16	
GNMA	11.29	N.L.+	.02
Grow Tr	16.02	N.L.+	.14
Govt Tr	10.41	N.L.+	
Hi Incm	12.74	13.63+	.03
Hi Yld	11.04	N.L.+	.02

Trst Sh			
Istel Fund			
Ivy Grwth			
Ivy InstInv			
JP Growth			
JP Income			
Janus Fund			
Jan Fnd			
Janus VI			
Janus Vn			
Jans			
John Hancoc			
Bond Fd			
Globl Tr			
Growth			
Spcl Eqt			
US GvSc			
Tax Ex			
USGG			
Kauf Fund			
Kemper			
Cal Tax			
Income			
Growth			
High Yld			
Int'l Fd			
Muni Bd			
Optn Inc			
Summit			
Technol			
Total R			
US GvSc			
KY Tax Fr			
Keystone			
Cust B1 r			
Cust B2 r			

when an estate has been created to replace income derived from the deceased.

The two major types of insurance are Term and Whole Life. There is also the hybrid of the two and that's a term policy with an investment component that's often called Universal Life. Term insurance is purely death coverage, the premiums increase with your age. There is no savings component. In Whole Life insurance the premiums are priced over time, therefore higher at the beginning to compensate for when you become older. There is a savings component, offering a small interest rate. Contrary to most customers' understanding, this savings is not added to the value of the policy and the customer is charged interest if they want to borrow "their money." I am a strong advocate of Term over Whole Life and the difference between what you would pay for Term Insurance, which is purely death coverage with no investment component and Whole Life or Universal Life should then be invested to continue to build your estate with the ultimate objective of eliminating the need for insurance completely. For example, a $25,000 Term Policy for a 30-year-old male may carry premiums of $300 a year on the average. The Whole Life Policy worth the same $25,000 a year may carry premiums of $600 with a cash value component. Listed below is the mathematical computation of what would happen if both parties died at 55 years of age.

Term Insurance
Costs $300 a yr x 25yrs = $7,500
Benefits= $25,000
CashValue = $17,500

Whole Life Insurance
Costs $600 a yr x25yrs= $15,000
Benefits= $25,000
Cash Value = $10,000
Savings = $5,000

Let's now review the above example. The applicant with Term Insurance only paid $7,500 versus Whole Life in which the person paid $15,000. This savings of $7,500 could then be invested into a money market, mutual fund, common stock, or real estate. The term premium may increase slightly in the latter years, but many policies are stable and hopefully you won't need it in the later years. The Whole Life applicant has $5,000 in savings, but when he died this was not added to the $25,000 policy. It was only available for borrowing. The applicant can earn a far greater return than the five percent that the insurance company says it will pay in Whole Life. Many insurance agents tell me the only reason they recommend Whole Life is because most people would not take advantage of the difference in premiums and invest it properly. I don't believe two wrongs make a right. It's a poor investment strategy and we should not be presumptuous in assuming that African Americans don't have enough sense to invest their money wisely.

It is not profitable to combine insurance and investments together. Insurance companies are excellent for their original intention. It would behoove everyone to simply pay less in insurance and have the wisdom and foresight to invest the difference properly. More importantly, insurance is designed only as a short term remedy, while the estate is being built. There should be no need for an older person to have to pay $1,000 and more per year in insurance if they had built an estate between the ages of 21 and 65. Remember, insurance was only designed to replace your income for your dependent. Over the course of time, your dependents should have been eliminated while your estate blossomed.

> If African Americans see that they have a future then they will begin to operate on the perspective that their children must continue the legacy. It is the parents' responsibility to transfer wealth over to them. It is important that African Americans design wills and trusts that can clearly explain how the fruits of their labor are going to be divided among their heirs. Only 20 percent of African Americans develop a will.[11]

It is important that this is done, because if it is not, the IRS can impound the assets and create a great degree of red tape and legal expense for family members to divide the assets properly. The first step is for African Americans to invest their money wisely so there will be something at the end of the rainbow. Secondly, it is imperative that the will or trust is designed to ensure the heirs will receive the money and not the government. It's demoralizing to see family members immediately after a funeral, argue and destroy an estate that the builder took a lifetime to create.

As we move into the next chapter on business development, please remember that 38 percent of the people that are wealthy secured their wealth through owning their own businesses. These businesses were not started overnight. They began with a vision. Large numbers of businesses started because people understood the concept of sales. I'd like to conclude this chapter and lead into the next, Starting Your Own Business, with the area of sales because it is an excellent way for a person who wants to build personal wealth to gain additional income with a part time position in sales. Success in this area can then lead into starting your own business.

Unfortunately, sales is another area where African Americans suffer because they operate from the perspective of the guarantee. Most African Americans would rather have a guaranteed salary of $20,000 than earning 10 to 50 percent commissions on an unlimited amount of sales. George Subira has written an excellent book titled *Getting Black Folks To Sell*. Listed below are attitudes he's observed concerning sales.

White Attitude Toward Sales

Selling is a great source of income; money is *everywhere*.

I don't want any *limit* put on how much money I can make.

I'm going to *learn* all I can about this product and the market and make a mint.

The reason I like this field is because I'm really *independent*. I make most of the decisions as long as I bring in the bottom line.

You know once you learn how to sell it's almost *impossible to be unemployed*; there are always openings in sales.

This field is great; I deal with people from *all over the world*-the Middle East, Africa, India, especially Japan and South Korea.

I started with that *desk full of applications* and 35 dollars in my pocket. Now I guess you can say I'm rich.

Black Attitude Toward Sales

You go broke selling;
nobody has any money.

I *need* a set salary so I
can see where I'm going.

I don't have the *gift of
gab to make it in sales.*

I can be a good worker,
just *tell me what to do*
and I'll do it.

The people I know in
sales *can't be doing that*
great; *every time you
look up, they're selling
something different.*

Hey, you know you can't
make any money dealing
with White folks; they
only spend it among
themselves.

Well you know what they
always say, it takes
money to make money.[12]

We need more businesses, especially those that give back to the community.

Chapter 7

Starting Your Own Business

We are charged by Christ to serve, and motivated by Imhotep and Garvey toward Black excellence; all for customers, who are the most important persons in this business.

African American Images Creed

BUSINESS COMMANDMENTS

A customer is the most important person in this business.

A customer is not dependent on us. We are dependent on him.

A customer is not an interruption.

A customer does us a favor when calling attention to our shortcomings.

A customer is part of our business, not an outsider.

A customer is not someone to argue or match wits with.

A customer is a person who brings us their wants. It is our job to fill these wants.

A customer is the life blood of this business.

Of all the business theories and strategies that are available to read and research, I believe the most important aspect of a business is the motive of the owner. People have different reasons for starting a business and oftentimes, regrettably, it is not satisfying customers. George Subira, in his book titled *Black Folks Guide to Making Big Money in America* points out that some business owners start a business because they want to be the boss and customer satisfaction is not high on their priority lists. If your objective and motive for starting a business is because you want to be in control, or so that you can open and close when you want to, or to determine what kind of product or service you want to provide for your customers without seeking any input from them, or to argue with customers about your policies, then it's almost assured that you will be a business failure. The ideal motive for starting a business is if there is something you enjoy making or providing that you have determined from official or unofficial market research has a reasonable degree of consumer demand. Additional motives are profits, consumer satisfaction, and increased employment in our community. There are many advantages to owning your own business such as:

- There is a greater potential for income.
- There is a greater utilization of all of your resources.
- There is a greater potential for flexible hours.
- There is a greater control of your destiny.
- There is a greater ability to pass wealth on to your children.
- There is a greater opportunity to employ family, friends, and community members.
- There is greater retirement security.
- There is greater reduction of tax liability.

Let's review some of the above advantages. I mentioned in a previous chapter that persons who own their own businesses have five times the net worth of those who are salaried employees. I also indicated that 98 percent of the people who earn over $50,000 own their businesses versus two percent that work for someone else. Unfortunately, in the African American community many people have become comfortable with a good job and would rather receive a guaranteed "salary" than deal with the possibility of unlimited income. Owning your business allows all of your human resources to be utilized. Oftentimes in corporate America, a person is "pigeon holed" into a particular department, but when you own your own business you can be involved in accounting, marketing, product development, sales, and public relations. You become multifaceted.

Another benefit is the potential for flexible hours. I stress potential because most business owners do work more total hours than they would as employees, but depending upon the nature of the business there is the possibility for greater flexibility. If your business is not retail you have the ability to determine your hours, and also have greater control of your destiny. Working for someone else places you in a dependent situation. You may be subject to poor judgement and bad business decisions. Owning your own business allows you the opportunity to have greater control of your destiny and places the future in your hands. I'm dismayed when African Americans talk about self-determination, but deep down inside feel more secure being on someone else's payroll, including the oppressor, than branching out on their own, starting their business, and having their future dependent on their own resources.

Entrepreneurship allows you the opportunity to pass greater wealth on to your children. It also empowers children to become a part of an institution and ultimately own it. Working 20, 30, and 40 years for someone else does not create ownership that can be passed on to future generations. We need people in the African American community that have the vision and foresight to build institutions. You can't pass a "good job" down to your offspring.

> Starting your own business also creates the opportunity to employ family members, friends, and members of the larger African American community. Eighty percent of the new jobs that are created in America are created by small businesses[1]

Most of these businesses are employing people who are in close proximity to them. I don't think a person can be viewed as being racist if he is the president of a business and employs three to ten people, and most of the employees are people who are within his family, community, and church. Owning your business also creates greater security for retirement. There is a much greater chance of creating wealth through ownership.

Lastly, entrepreneurship permits for greater flexibility on taxes because of the increased number of areas that can be utilized for write-offs. Wealth derived solely from salaries does not provide the same number of opportunities for tax write-offs as income derived from ownership. While there are numerous advantages to owning your own business there are also numerous disadvantages which include:

• Long Hours
• Possibility for Low Pay
• Additional Responsibilities
• A Negative View from the Community Toward Business Ownership
• The Pressures of Providing Customer Satisfaction

While business owners have five times the net worth of those who work for someone they also work 10 to 20 hours more than the average salaried employee. This not only creates an additional strain on the individual, but this also can hold negative implications for child rearing and marital stability. While owning your own business provides an opportunity for unlimited income, it also has the reverse dilemma of unlimited losses. In addition, at the outset of business formation most business owners receive a small salary. This can also create financial difficulties especially if they left a "good job" with a "good salary" because it requires an alteration in lifestyle. Also, most employees are able to work an eight hour day and leave the responsibilities at the office; when you become a business owner very seldom do you ever leave the responsibilities at the office, they are taken to the bedroom, living room, and the bathroom.

In the chapter Obstacles To Black Economic Development, I mentioned that there's often a negative view from the community about business ownership. Unfortunately, in the African American community the person who is an engineer is revered more than a person who owns a laundromat. Superficially, it appears that the engineer is very successful with a good job paying upwards of $40,000. People may not know that the owner of a laundromat could be making over a $100,000 , employing several members of his family, and able to pass the institution on to future generations. The negative stereotype of business owners does not encourage African Americans to start their own business. The second issue I want to examine is the personality traits of the owner - not everyone is suited for entrepreneurship. Listed below are questions that everyone should honestly ask themselves before embarking on starting a business.

- Are you a risk-taker?
- Are you a hard worker?
- Are you a self-starter?
- Can you make sound decisions under pressure?
- Do you possess good organizational skills?
- Do you have good communication skills?
- Are you constantly upgrading your skills and attending workshops and seminars to keep abreast of current trends?

- Do you set and accomplish your goals within budget and time limitations?
- Are you resilient and do you value diversity?

These are just some of the many characteristics of a successful entrepreneur. It is advantageous to possess all of these traits. When that is not possible, it is equally important to acknowledge your shortcomings and limitations and have other staff members fill that void. In many business discussions, classes, and articles, capital is considered the most important resource in the business. I disagree, I feel that the most important resource to the business is the personnel followed by the product and then capital. Institutions, whether educational, political, cultural, or business oriented start with good leadership. Effective principals can produce high achieving schools and effective presidents produce profitable businesses.

An effective business owner is a risk taker and has a high level of self-esteem. Most people who have a moderate or low level of self esteem play by the odds and are very concerned about what other people would think of their failure. Consequently, their own personal goals, desires, and dreams are seldom fulfilled because they are afraid of taking a risk. I am in no way endorsing an entrepreneur to act like a gambler and role the dice. I reiterate, business owners should align themselves with sound critical thinkers.

Les Brown, in one of his speeches raises the question, What is it that you want so much that you'll spend literally every waking hour thinking about it, over meals pondering it, and when sleeping dreaming about it? Successful people are able to harness all of their energy and focus it on their objective. People that are risk takers, with strong self-esteem, who are intense, clearly focused, and have a business acumen may be short financially, but possess "social capital" which I feel is more important.

I believe there is a distinction between being an owner and a manager. Managers have the technical skills to run and operate someone else's corporation. Many African Americans perform this role. They have advanced degrees from prestigious universities, and they're doing an excellent job of managing someone elses business, but many of them do not have the training, guts, nor desire to start their own corporation. As a result, in the African American community we have a mismatch with many members possessing skills to operate a business, but choosing not to, and conversely, members who have the guts, but don't have business acumen. Consequently, we have large numbers of business failures.

Becoming business literate does not require a formal degree, but I strongly encourage it. When I was developing my business I had a BA in Economics, but I chose to continue my education and eventually secured a Doctorate in Business Administration. I felt acquiring theory was important, but I also value the experience via internships and working as an employee in the industry of your preference. Many business failures could have been avoided if the owners had acquired the skills or understood their limitations and surrounded themselves with good accountants, lawyers, bankers, and marketing representatives. Many owners tell me that they can't afford an accountant, lawyer, and a marketing representative, and don't feel that bankers are interested in their operations. I don't think any entrepreneur brings to the table all the skills of this diversified group.

I would be remiss if I did not provide some comments about whether spouses, relatives, and friends should be partners or staff members in the business. There have been many business casualties that have ended in divorce. There's a rule by some that says, "Good friends make poor business partners." Like oil and water, business and social relationships simply do not mix. The problem is one of emotions. Family relationships and friendships are based on emotional ties. That is not the criteria which should be used in making decisions for business. It appears that foreigners have been able to place business over personal, emotional, and sometimes petty issues.

George Subira devotes a major section in *Black Folks Guide To Business Success* to the complexity of husbands and wives working together. Some of the factors that Subira acknowledges in this area include, the fear of risk, losing a guaranteed income, possibility of not working in the area of your degree, a decline in lifestyle, lack of consensus, reduction of time toward domestic responsibility and children, and ego. I mentioned earlier that one of the most important characteristics of being an entrepreneur is being a risk taker and yet this may not be accepted by the spouse.

> The entrepreneur may be a risk taker but the spouse is not. This can create a great degree of tension in the business and family. I often feel this creates no win situations. If the project fails then the spouse can continue to reiterate that it was too big of a risk and say, "I told you so."[2]

If it succeeds then they benefit from the situation, but still have problems with the extent of the risk.

I mentioned earlier the concept of a "good job." For many people the wise thing to do is to keep a guaranteed income rather than taking a chance on earning an unlimited income. Many business owners have degrees in other areas and oftentimes parents and spouses would prefer for them to remain in the area of their formal education. Engineers and accountants, etc., should not own laundromats and grocery stores, is the view held by some people. When a spouse leaves a "good job" where they were making $40,000 and starts a business where for the first few years they only earn 10 to 20,000 requires an adjustment in the budget and lifestyle. This can create tension in a marriage especially if the other spouse was not in agreement with the initial decision. Some men say they want their wives to start their own business as long as their dinner will be on the table at six o'clock, and the children bathed and in bed by eight o'clock. Some women say they want their husbands to be assertive and exert leadership, but on the job, not "doing for self."

The last problem previously cited in families has to deal with ego and security. Men have more of the former and women want more of the latter. Many men have problems if women earn more than they do and this can easily result with unlimited income. Many men have lost their dreams and their spirits have been broken because their wives wanted them to play it by the odds for security.

Please note there is a distinction between spouses that are supporting each other in the development of a business and spouses working together. My comments have been about the former. It is more complex if they are working together. This requires greater understanding and acceptance. Most studies illustrate that to be effective there needs to be clear job descriptions, so both have adequate space. Friendships, while not as volatile as family relationships also can be burdensome if decisions are made based on emotion rather than business logic.

The criteria on who should be your business partner should be based on complementing your strengths and weaknesses not friendship.

The second most important aspect in the development of the business after the personnel is the product or service. Many people think that they have a business because the wife cooks very well. There is more to market research than the family asking for seconds on dessert. The food business is very competitive and many establishments offer buffets at bargain prices. It is very difficult for Bob's Cafe and Betty's Grill to compete against institutions of a substantially larger magnitude. In the African American community there are many restaurants that were started purely because it was determined among family members that he or she was a very good cook, they loved to do it, and it would make a worthwhile business. I believe the best place to start the determination of what product or service you want to provide should be based on something that you like to make or do. In this regard, your business will not feel like work because you enjoy it. It is an excellent situation when you have the opportunity to produce or provide a service that you probably would have provided for someone anyway because of your affinity. I know personally, being an avid reader and someone who likes to write, speak, and share ideas, that I am very thankful that the communications business that I own allows me an opportunity to do what I would have done on my free time as a hobby.

George Subira suggests with his book *Getting Black Folks To Sell* that all of us could start a business by simply asking ourselves what are the products we like and identifying the manufacturers of those products and selling them.

Many people who do not identify with sales would be greatly surprised if they sold an item they personally use. It's much easier distributing an item that you personally consume. As I mentioned previously, just because you like that product or that service does not mean there is an adequate consumer demand to turn the selling of this product into a business. Ideally speaking, there will be a perfect union between your desires and consumer demand. I am very much aware there is a greater demand in the African American community for dope and liquor than for books. Obviously, I choose not to sell liquor and dope because the criteria for starting a business is not solely based on consumer demand, but it needs to be considered. If a person chooses to provide a product or service where the consumer demand is as low as it is in this country for books, then a business owner is going to have to develop a marketing strategy to stimulate and acknowledge the possibility of lower sales.

I learned I was not in the book publishing business, but the communication industry which consists of the dissemination of ideas. While there is not a large demand for books, there is a large demand for ideas; which can be dispersed through books, but also presented in speeches, audio and video tapes, computer software, curriculum, and full-feature films. Listed below are a collection of businesses to stimulate your final decision based on a combination of factors: interest, ability, capital reqiure requirements, consumer demand, and profitability.

1) Real Estate
2) Printing
3) Travel Agency
4) General Repairs
5) Office and Home Cleaning Service
6) Foam Manufacturer
7) Indoor Amusement Park
8) Financial Broker
9) Food Delivery Service
10) Landscaping
11) Moving
12) Video Taping
13) Day Care
14) Health and Fitness Center
15) Interior Decorating

Many people feel that the major reason for the lack of development of Black businesses is because of a lack of capital. It is not that I underestimate this very important part of business formation and growth, but I feel that people and product development are essential and without them there will be no need for capital. I do acknowledge that after people and product development the business can not grow without the generation of capital. I think the best place to begin pondering the creation of capital is in college. While so many other students are majoring in Omega Psi Phi, Delta Sigma Theta, Bid Whist, and partying, I think it's important for African Americans to identify those majoring in accounting, marketing, and engineering and begin the formation of their business. This group can begin serious planning of a business while in college and create a savings account ever so small. The members may choose to work for corporate America for one to five years and develop a budget based on needs rather than wants. The difference between what they are paid and their needs can also be placed in the savings account and over a period of time will allow for the capitalization of the business.

Working for corporate America and living off needs and investing the difference sounds very simple, but many people especially African Americans have found this very difficult to achieve. For some the problem was a lukewarm desire to start their own business and becoming more secure in corporate America. For others, the problem has been their inability to resist commercials that promote materialism. Many college students have used their first few checks to buy an expensive car and wardrobe. This delays their plans of starting their business. It is also important that if this is going to be the avenue for capital development that the monies are placed in an account that has a competitive rate of return and are liquidable enough so they can be used at any time for business formation. The traditional approach is to contact the bank. There is contradiction between entrepreneurs and bankers because entrepreneurs are initiating a business where there are risks involved. This is in contrast with bankers who want risk free loans supported with collateral.

The most successful way to secure loans from the bank is to predict bankers' questions and concerns. Bankers are looking for businesses where the owners have invested a portion of their own equity into the business. Secondly, they are looking for people who have sound credit histories, collateral to support the loan, personnel that has the experience and training to operate a successful business, and a business plan that demonstrates a clear understanding of the industry, competition, and product strengths and weaknesses. With that in mind, it becomes imperative that the loan applicant provides a business plan or a loan proposal that clearly spells out the purpose of the loan, the description of the business, a management profile, financial statements, and sources of collateral.

Another area of funding that is often overlooked is through the state and the various departments which include: The Department of Commerce, The Small Business Administration, The Department of Revenue, and The Department of Community Affairs. Most states have allocated monies for "minority groups." These loans often charge lower interest rates. Many of these loans require an illustration that the monies will generate additional employment within the state. These loans can often be used with other loans from private institutions. Several of these departments also provide technical assistance in the preparation of the loan application. Numerous banks are more willing to loan applicants money when they know the state is a participant.

This chapter is an attempt to describe on a general basis the ways to start a business. In the last chapter, Black Economic Empowerment, we will provide a comprehensive strategy on how we can address the capital problem that many African American entrepreneurs are experiencing. The buzz word in the business industry is the "business plan." Unfortunately, if you ask Black business people do they have a business plan, and if so when was the last time they looked at it, that would probably confirm why so many of our businesses are not doing better. The discussion about business plans seems to occur more from neophytes and people who are pondering the possibility than from existing business owners. Some people erroneously think that business plans are only to be developed for bankers and that they would not be necessary if you had an adequate amount of capital to start your business or if you are already in operation. They think that it is not necessary to refer to a business plan throughout the life of the business. These assumptions couldn't be further from the truth. A business plan is the road map that the business owner will use, not only in developing a proposal for a bank, but also for the business owner to utilize for better decision making.

I acknowledge that many African Americans are oral people and right brain thinkers, and that oftentimes the business plan is in the owners' heads. They can articulate it if asked the various questions that constitute a business plan, but they don't have it in writing. It is advantageous to place this business plan in writing. I think it crystallizes some of the ideas, objectives, and procedures. It also helps additional staff members to become more cognizant and aware of the business procedures not only when the business owner is alive, but in lieu of an untimely death. A plan also will allow additional staff members to know the general operating procedures. The basic outline for a business plan includes the following:

I.   Cover Sheet
II. Statement of Purpose
III. Table of Contents
IV. Description of the Business
V.   The Market
VI. Competition
VII. Location of the Business
VIII. Management
IX. Personnel
X.   Financial Data
XI. Balance Sheets
XII. Income Statements
XIII. Cash Flow Statements
XIV. Resumes

A comprehensive business plan should answer the following questions:

11) What is the business?
12) What market do you intend to service?
13) Why can you service that market better than your competition?
14) Why have you chosen your particular location?
15) What management and other personnel are available and required for this business?
16) Who is your market?
17) What is the present size of the market?
18) What percent of the market will you have?
19) What is the market's growth potential?
10) How are you going to satisfy your market?

11) How are you going to price your product or service?

12) How did you arrive at your price?

13) Is your price profitable?

14) Who are your five nearest competitors?

15) How will your operation be better than theirs?

16) How is their business?

17) How are their operations similar and dissimilar to yours?

18) What are their strengths and/or weaknesses?

19) What have you learned from watching their operation?

20) What is the present status of the neighborhood of your business?

21) How close is the business to bus lines, transportation, and parking facilities?

22) Is street traffic fairly heavy all day and in the evening?

Most present business owners have never formally asked themselves these questions. Ironically, many business owners may know the answers to most of these questions, but have not benefitted from the questions and the answers because they never formalized their operation into a business plan. Corrective adjustments could be made with the acquisition of this information. Other buzz words in the industry are the four P's of a business. They are Product, Price, Promotion, and Place of distribution. A successful business needs to first provide a quality product that is priced competitively, promoted well within the market place, and conveniently located for purchase. Any one of the four P's that has not been sufficiently addressed can be a detriment to the business. A high-quality product that is available at numerous outlets, well promoted, but is overpriced will not be successful. A product that is of high-quality, competitively priced, well promoted, but difficult to find will not be successful. A product that is all over town, well promoted and competitively priced, but lacking in quality will not be successful. These four P's are interdependent and it is essential that business owners understand the need for a business plan, and a full understanding of the four P's.

I have also observed, over the years, an imbalance in the three major areas of a business. These areas are product development, accounting, and marketing. Most business owners are schooled in one of these three areas and unfortunately, if they are not aware of the necessity for the other two to be developed, then their company will be top-heavy in one of the three categories. For example: If a business has an owner who comes from an accounting background, this business may not see the need to advertise and may have strict credit procedures. This makes it very difficult for sales to be made because of their strict accounting background. On the other hand, a company that has a business owner, who has more of a marketing orientation may be very lax in the area of credit and collection.

Unfortunately, many businesses, when capital is scarce, will state they don't have any money to advertise. They've allocated their money in production and accounting, but they have not allotted money for marketing. I believe that if you can't afford to advertise you can't afford to be in business. In the overall American economy, Americans have not placed the kind of money into research and development that's necessary for product quality and development. Consequently, they've allowed foreign competitors a greater share. Blue-chip businesses assign an equitable distribution of resources to product development, accounting, and marketing.

Because so many African Americans open retail operations, I can't stress enough the word location, location, and location. This is the most important component of a retail operation. There are many African American businesses that simply are in neighborhoods that are not conducive for growth and development. The decision to start your own business is very complex. Many people make the decision when they are in school, upon graduation, while working in corporate America, and when laid-off or fired. Some have started their own businesses in their homes. There are an estimated 13 million people who do some of their work at home for their employers and three million have decided to operate their business from home.[3]

This avenue reduces transportation time, there is a tremendous reduction in overhead, and it allows for personal benefits. Many people make the transition from employee to employer by starting off part time. Statistically, its difficult to identify and determine the accurate numbers of African Americans that have a part time business in their homes. This group is highly educated and their businesses are very stable. Unfortunately, the largest entrants into the business sector, cited by Timothy Bates, are people pursuing the retail and non-professional service sectors with little education and a much higher attrition rate. In the last chapter on Empowerment, more will be said about how the African American community could benefit if they increased the number of highly educated and professional members to start or develop full time ventures.

A concept that has received rave reviews is the incubator program. The concept of an incubator is where a supporting institution secures a building, and within the building will provide businesses with access to computers, typewriters, accountants, lawyers, printing facilities, and other technical assistance. Incubators operate off the principle of Ujamaa (cooperative economics), the sharing of expenses. It is not necessary for several businesses to each pay rent, buy computers, typewriters, legal and accounting fees, etc. When I first started my company in 1980, I was unofficially in an incubator program because Afro-Am allowed me to place my business inside of theirs; they allowed me to grow within that context for the first four years. Afro-Am provided me with space, telephone, copier, secretarial assistance, technical advice, inventory space, etc. This allowed me to develop the capital base necessary for future growth and development.

There are approximately 4200 businesses that presently operate within incubators. There are approximately 350 incubators in America. The average number of businesses per incubator is twelve. Businesses stay within an incubator for one to three years. Eighty percent of the businesses that were in incubators succeed within three to five years versus 25 percent of other businesses. In addition, 84 percent of the businesses that were in incubators remain in the community.

Universities sponsor 17 percent of the incubators, another 39 percent are financed by economic development organizations and governmental agencies. Fourteen percent are financed by for profit institutions that operate very similar as venture capitalists. The remaining 30 percent have multiple sponsors or some other type of funding.[4]

It is unfortunate that foreigners and the incubator program see more value in Ujamaa than the people that gave the principle to the world. Further information about incubators can be secured from the National Business Incubation Association located in Athens, Ohio. I think it is very impressive that with the large numbers of business failures, the utilization of incubators is one way that we can increase the survival rate of businesses. An 80 percent success rate and remaining in the community is also appealing for community empowerment.

Another way to start your own business and increase the survival rate is by being involved in a franchise. They have been much more successful than businesses that have started from scratch, especially by parties that did not have a business plan and did not have a strong educational background. The franchise industry is a very large industry estimated at 700 billion dollars.

There are approximately 500,000 franchises and African Americans only own 10,142 or approximately two percent. Eighteen percent of the franchises are in the fast food area, but areas where there are tremendous growth would be business services, automobile repairs and services, home care and maintenance, weight control centers, and hair salons.[5]

While the success ratio is higher for franchise owners than for regular businesses, people should be very careful about thinking that owning a franchise is 100 percent foolproof. People who are interested in this area should secure a clear definition of their personal liability and obligations as a franchisee. They should know who is responsible for the selection of the franchise, what their renewal rights are, under what terms are you allowed or required to terminate the agreement, and are they required to purchase goods and services from the franchise company or other specific suppliers. Avoid franchise companies that provide little or no training in how to run a franchise, and carefully study all legal documents especially the Uniform Franchise Offering Circular (UFOC) which provides detailed information about the franchises. These documents should be reviewed with an attorney. Preferably one that has experience in franchise agreements.

Franchising of course is not for everyone. A person whose going to be involved in a franchise needs to be a team player. This structure will not allow you to determine the kinds of products or services you will provide, nor will it allow you to develop your own advertising strategy, decor, and other kinds of decisions that other owners are able to make. It is an excellent opportunity for someone who wants to minimize risk and someone who is not adamant about being independent. As mentioned earlier, it has a much higher retention rate. In the last chapter, Black Economic Empowerment, we will discuss the fact that while franchises are significant, they are institutions owned by someone else, and we simply are allowed the opportunity to secure a piece of their pie.

The last area I want to look at in this chapter, Starting Your Own Business is the issue of governmental set - asides, the SBA, and The Minority Purchasing Council. Many businesses have been able to start because they have secured contracts from either local, state, or federal government. The government has always been a much fairer source than private enterprise with regards to allocating monies for minority vendors. The Fortune 500 companies spent approximately 15 billion dollars in 1990 with 'minority' firms, but this is a small portion of the 420 billion dollars that was spent by the top 100 corporations alone.

> In the chapter on the present status of the economy we looked at some of the implications of the current set - aside program, for example, The Department of Defense has legislation requiring that five percent of all of their contracts go to minority owned firms and this is worth annually, on the average 150 billion dollars.[6]

However, this too has some major ramifications. Some we discussed in Chapter six with regards to some recent court decisions that have reversed some of the set - aside programs. In addition, the way the government defines minority includes women. As a result, large numbers of

White companies owned by men simply are creating new firms using their wives and female relatives as "minorities."

> They are rationalizing that this is now a minority firm and securing multi-million dollar contracts. In Chicago for example, female contractors came away with nine million dollars worth of construction contracts of the 210 million dollar Dan Ryan Expressway. This was triple the amount awarded to Black firms.[7]

This was not the original intention of how these programs were to be used. Some newly created firms are 'salt and pepper' corporations. White men use minorities as "fronts" to satisfy the pepper requirement, while the monies and decisions are made by the salt. Secondarily, the paperwork for filling out these applications can be mind boggling and for the small firm that is dependent upon this contract many times they simply can not survive the paperwork.

> Thirdly, according to the General Accounting Office, the SBA Program has 2,938 participants in which 1,498 are Black, but 1,225 of these firms reported no SBA business in 1987. Another 555 did less than $100,000.00.[8]

My recommendation in the utilization of these programs is very similar to my strategy regarding grants. Payroll and rent should not be dependent upon a grant and you should not have a major portion of your budget dependent on governmental set - asides. There are delays for contract approval which can be catastrophic to cash flow. There is also a component of the legislation where firms at some point are supposed to graduate, this can be very detrimental to a company that has become exclusively dependent on governmental contracts.

I do feel that we need African American businesses pursuing public and private sector contracts. Reginald Lewis was able to use the MESBIC to eventually acquire Beatrice Foods. It is an excellent area to pursue as long as we understand some of the pitfalls that accompany the endeavor. It is now time to move from theory to practice and empower our people economically. The final chapter awaits you.

We need to "do for self" by building an economic base.

Chapter 8

Black Economic Empowerment

In this last and most important chapter, "Black Economic Empowerment," I have asked some of my closest friends and people who have devoted a great degree of their time toward the liberation of our people, specifically in the economic arena, to help me with this last chapter. These men and women come from a diverse background. Some are nationalists, others are mainstream, but they all, in my opinion, have contributed greatly to the discussion of economic development and empowerment. The people who have helped me greatly in writing this book and who I'm inviting to this "mock" meeting include the following: 1) John Raye, founder and president of Majestic Eagles. Raye feels that the major problem with the small number of African American businesses is not a lack of capital or expertise but self-doubt and low self-esteem. 2) John Jacobs, executive director for the National Urban League. John Jacobs believes that the plight of the Black community is very similar to what happened in Eastern Europe and believes that just as America created a Marshall and MacArthur Plan for the revitalization of foreign countries that this same type of plan is needed in the inner cities of America. 3) Reginald Lewis, chief executive officer of Beatrice Foods, the largest Black owned business in the country with sales exceeding one billion dollars. 4) Jesse Jackson, who believes one of the best ways to stimulate economic growth in the community is greater utilization of pension funds. These pension funds could either come from larger unions nationwide or Black unions where these monies presently are being invested outside the Black community and should be invested to stimulate growth within the African American community. 5) Tony Brown, architect of the Buy Freedom Campaign who also developed a Black consumer hotline that will allow businesses and consumers to talk with each other and the proceeds from the 900 hotline are to be used to finance additional businesses and create scholarships for college bound youth. 6) Derric Price, founder of Afro Dollars, a concept where a new currency has been devised (one, five, 10, and 20 dollar bills) with the pictures of famous

African Americans on the dollar. This program allows businesses to receive Afro dollars from consumers and turn them back into banks that have agreed to accept this new currency. Proceeds from the use of the currency will also create additional businesses and provide low income housing and loans for students. 7) Benjamin Hooks, executive director of the NAACP who also believes in a similar idea with the utilization of the two dollar bill. A concept where African Americans on a certain day of the year will use the two dollar bill to indicate to the entire country the tremendous buying power of African Americans. 8) Rev. Al Sampson, officer of the National Black Farmers' Harvest. He's developed a strategy to bring together the Southern farmer and the Northern consumer. Rev. Sampson believes that it makes no sense for African Americans to pay higher prices for food in the north and for many to go without, while simultaneously Black farmers are becoming extinct because they can not find a market for their products. 9) John Johnson, chief executive officer of the Johnson Publishing Company, the second largest business in Black America, and publisher of *Ebony* magazine with the largest circulation in Black America. 10) Ed Gardner, chief executive officer of Soft Sheen which is the sixth largest business in Black America and the largest African American manufacturer which has now expanded its operations to Europe and Africa. 11) Earl Graves, publisher of *Black Enterprise Magazine*. A journal devoted to exploring the issues of Black economic development. 12) Joshua Smith, chief executive officer of the Maxima Corporation and the director for the Commission on Minority Business Development. 13) George Frazier, publisher of *Success Guide Magazine.* An organ designed to expose the large number of successful African Americans and businesses within the community with the sole objective of networking. 14) Parren Mitchell, former congressman and architect of legislation creating setasides from the federal government to benefit "minority firms." 15) Louis Farrakhan, minister of the Nation of Islam. Under the teaching of Elijah Muhammad, he has been a strong advocate of economic development, producing Power products, baked goods, fish, and the newspaper *The Final Call.* He also has advocated a separate land base. 16) Officers would also be invited from the Deal Organization. A company that has designed a catalogue with hundreds of Black manufacturers displaying their product and allowing consumers to purchase from a national collective. 17) The Black United Fund, an organization that attempts to receive contributions that can be invested into the community in a similar manner to the United Way. 18) Officers are also invited from Black Expo whose effort is designed to bring vendors from around the country together, all under one roof, to display their wares. 19) Officers are also invited from the companies that have developed the *Black Pages*. A local telephone directory categorizing Black businesses by areas. 20) Officers from the Shrine of the Black Madonna, a very progressive, religious, and social organization based in Atlanta, Detroit, Houston, and Kalamazoo that has developed churches, bookstores, housing complexes, and farms for the liberation of African American people. 21) Congressman John Conyers, attorney Nkechi Taifa, and the National Coalition of Blacks for Reparations in America. This organization now has in congressional committee a bill to seriously explore the need for reparations for African Americans for the years of free labor that Africans were forced to give to America. 22) An officer from the Hebrew Israelites, a religious cultural organization with various businesses in cities in America, who have also secured land and has developed communities in Israel and Ghana. 23) Representing the media are Robert Johnson, chief executive officer of Black Entertainment Television and Emerge magazine. 24) Bob Law, national talk show host for the widely heralded show, "Night Talk." Edward Lewis, publisher of *Essence* magazine. The Professors will include: David Swinton, Julianne Malveaux, Andrew Brimmer, H. Naylor Fitzhugh, and Sybil Mobley. The writers will include: George Subira, Robert Browne, Robert Woodson, John Butler, Shelly Greene, Paul Pryde, Timothy Bates, Earl Ofari Hutchinson, and myself.

I'm sure that we could have another meeting with just as many talented men and women who also are needed to address the serious issue of economic empowerment. I simply chose some of my closest friends, and men and women who have contributed greatly over the years in discussing the economic issues affecting our community. The first objective that we need to achieve at this meeting is to agree that we will leave the ego at the door. If we're going to be successful with this body, we will have to leave the ego at the door and accept the fact that we all have different views on solving the problem. They can only be solved if we work together. Secondly, we need to discuss our assets. As a committee, we earned last year close to $300 billion. We have approximately 40 million Africans living in America. We primarily reside in the 30 largest markets in America. We have greater than one million African Americans who possess college degrees, more than any other country. We own close to four million acres of land. We have approximately 6,000 elected officials. We have an estimated 60,000 churches which 16 million people attend at some time or another. We are the major participants in athletics and in entertainment. We have great market penetration in the hair care industry. Rev. Sampson feels soul food has the greatest potential to be exported.

In previous chapters, we also looked at some of our weaknesses. Presently, Whites have an average wealth of $39,000 per household and we have an average wealth of $3,400 dollars per household. Our income ratio is only 57 percent of Whites'. Thirty-three percent of our race lives below the poverty line. Forty-two percent of our 17-year-olds can't read beyond a sixth-grade reading level. We have 609,000 African American men in prison. One out of every four African American males at some point will be involved with the penal institution. In terms of business start-ups per thousand, we only develop nine businesses per thousand African Americans. This is far below all other groups including Hispanics, Asians, and Whites who start 64 per thousand. Most of our businesses are marginal, 83 percent have no employees and annual sales average $11,400.

Before we discuss individual proposals at this meeting we need to make sure that we all know why we are here. We are here because we have the same goal. The objective of this meeting is to determine how we can employ as many African American men and women who are old enough and eligible to work. This meeting is not designed for a few parties to become millionaires. Presently, 25 percent of our race makes over 40,000 dollars, 33 percent of our race lives below the poverty line. As was previously stated, under the Jackson/Young administration in Atlanta numerous contracts were won by Black entrepreneurs during the building of the airport. This created numerous Black millionaires, but Atlanta has one of the highest concentrations of Black poverty of any city in the country. At the same time I don't want theoreticians to indict people like Reginald Lewis, John

Johnson, and Ed Gardner when they have not used any of their theories to employ anyone.

In looking at the proposals that were submitted by all the people who are here at this meeting, I attempted to categorize them and determine the top five proposals to present to the entire body. The top five proposals were in business development, product promotion and distribution, capital formation, segmented marketing, and reparations. The first area is business formation. I carefully looked at the work of Timothy Bates, Shelly Greene, Paul Pryde, John Butler, George Subira, Robert Woodson, The Howard University Entrepreneur Program, The Majestic Eagles, and myself. There were a number of similar ideas that came from the group that we could share with the larger public on business formation. I developed a concept called the Ujamaa Meeting. I conduct a community meeting and there are certain rules established. The first rule is that everyone has to bring $100 to the meeting. The second is that everyone has to bring a business plan. The third rule is that everyone agrees whoever has the best business plan after the presentation and the vote will receive all the monies that were collected from the participants. The fourth rule is that the person who receives the money will attempt to do as much business as possible with the existing people inside this room. We will then meet the following month and repeat the procedures until as many people as possible have now received the monies from this group to start their own businesses.

Timothy Bates points out in his latest book on Black Enterprises, there are two types of firms, "traditional" and "emerging." The owner of the former has less education and capital, is concentrated in retail and service industries, and is located in the community. The emerging has greater education and capital, is involved more in wholesaling and professional services, and is located in the expanding community or central business district. Bates acknowledges that we have more traditional than emerging firms and the latter is larger and more profitable. College - educated African Americans should learn from the above research, and start businesses, rather than working for the government or corporate America. John Butler, Shelly Greene, and Paul Pryde also provide a great degree of historical and contemporary case studies of how African Americans were able to start their own businesses, and do very well despite discrimination. John Butler illustrates how the enclave was a response to discrimination. The Majestic Eagles provide a support service to perspective entrepreneurs. A person attending the meeting will find like-minded people in attendance who will give encouragement, technical assistance, discounted prices for products and services, and often financial assistance. In a previous chapter, I also mentioned that there is an 80 percent success rate if the business is housed within an incubator. An equally high success rate exists in franchises.

The last item that the writers and professors wanted to offer in this first area of business formation is that African American businesses can not rely on racial loyalty as the leading criteria for support of their businesses. Research shows that African American consumers respond more to price and quality than racial loyalty. Therefore, it behooves the African American business to concentrate more on price and quality and if, because of market factors and monopoly capitalism, it's difficult to compete against K-Mart and Sears on price, it does not preclude the opportunity to compete against other businesses in the area of service.

The second proposal that we want to look at is product promotion and distribution. There were numerous people in this room who presented proposals that we categorized in the area of product promotion and distribution. The Deal Organization, *Success Guide Magazine*, Black Expo, Black Pages Telephone Directories, Tony Brown's Buy Freedom Campaign, The Buyers Hotline, and Afro Dollars are all programs and strategies with the major objective being the desire to reach the 40 million African Americans and the 300 billion dollars we earned.

The Deal Organization has developed a catalogue of Black manufacturers with the hopes that if people see the catalogue they may order through direct mail to secure their products. Tony Brown's Hotline has an identical objective only through telemarketing. Black Expos are designed to have people walk through convention sites and become more aware of Black products and either buy them directly or through future orders. The Buy Freedom Campaign and Afro Dollars are designed to identify businesses that have made a commitment to Black economic development. The *Black Pages* is an attempt through print to develop a telephone directory that will also increase the exposure of Black products. *The Success Guide* is an opportunity to expose the community to successful African Americans and also businesses at the local level. All of these are strategies to reach the African American consumer. All of these are noble but do not compete very well against multinational companies like Nike and Pepsi that have access to our people through network and cable television, radio, print advertisement and chain stores.

As I previously pointed out, if you take a glance at *Ebony* and *Essence Magazines* you can count the number of Black businesses that were able to take out a full page ad on one hand and have four fingers left. If we are going to achieve parity in America, African American businesses have got to secure access to *Ebony, Essence,* and BET. This will mean that appeals need to be made to Robert Johnson at BET, John Johnson at *Ebony,* and Edward Lewis at *Essence Magazine* to see what can be done to expose a larger number of Black products to the Black consumer. If the objective is what can we do to employ the largest number of African Americans one of the things that we're going to have to do is to be able to share with each other. It also means that many businesses need to look at cooperative advertising to be able to afford the reduced prices for *Ebony, Essence,* BET, and Black radio. It also means that even though Ebony has a circulation of 1.8 million, *Essence* has a circulation of approximately 900,000, and BET may be in approximately 50 percent of African American homes there is much more we can do to support those organizations and others.

This second area is very significant because it appears that there is not a shortage of Black products but that the greatest problem is in promotion and distribution. There are African Americans who have produced Black underwear, barbecue sauce, deodorant, and anything else imaginable. Their greatest difficulty is in promotion and distribution which presently is being controlled largely outside of the African American community. A book could be allocated on the area of product promotion and distribution. I secured a Ph.D. in business administration with the accent on marketing because I knew its significance. We can not allow a situation where we have quality Black products that are not being consumed by African Americans just because they can not afford the $800,000 to advertise on the Superbowl Game,

$250,000 to advertise on the Bill Cosby Show, $125,000 to advertise on the Arsenio Hall Show, and $35,000 to advertise in *Ebony Magazine*. It has also become unfortunate that many African American consumers require that type of promotional strategy in order to motivate them to make the purchase. A prime example is what occurred with our movie, "Up Against the Wall."

We did very well, but we simply did not have the five to ten million dollar advertising budget of other companies. If African American consumers need a Dick Tracy, Terminator II, and New Jack City advertising budget in order to make a decision it means that many African American companies will not reach their full potential. It becomes important that we simultaneously support Black communication organizations to increase their circulation, viewership, and listenership while at the same time we need to have those organizations make themselves more accessible to African American businesses. African American businesses can enhance their success as mentioned earlier with cooperative advertising.

The third area that we need to look at is capital formation. Another book could be developed on the lack of support from Black banks for Black business development. Sometimes you wonder if these loan officers think the money is theirs and not the community depositors'. It is very discouraging for community residents to support Black banks when the banks have a modus operandi where they will receive community money and will invest the money in mutual funds and other large instruments but not back into the community. The development of a Black economic base mandates that we have the total support of Black banks. I just don't know how a bank can expect a new business at its inception to have liquid collateral for a loan dollar for dollar. If a new business had the $100,000 to invest it would not need to borrow $100,000 from a bank. At the same time, I'm very much aware of the plight of the banking industry, the lack of solvency and the numerous bank closings. On the whole, Black banks have been able to do a much better job than White banks and Savings and Loans, on the verge of bankruptcy or a bailout. There precludes additional room for improvement.

There are numerous suggestions that have been brought to the table by the people around this room. One of them has been The One Dollar Theory-if every African American and even the homeless gave one dollar; we would have forty million dollars. This proposal doesn't seem to have an economic flaw. We have the numbers and the money. The problem has always been do we see ourselves as a people? Do we feel it is significant enough, do we trust each other? How will we enforce the execution of this idea? These remain obstacles, but it is a very sound economic idea that all African Americans send one dollar to a designated organization. I'm recommending the National Black United Fund, there is no need to create a new organization.

When I was interviewed on a radio talk show, callers mentioned that they would not have a problem contributing to an organization if they felt that the people in the organization were respectable, trustworthy, and some suggested financially secure. I have the confidence based upon the track record of the Black United Fund to recommend this organization to receive the money, but because of the sensitivity that some people have on who they would trust, I'm recommending five additional people be designated to the committee at the National Black United Fund to administer this account. Those persons are Ed Gardner, the chief executive officer of Soft Sheen, this man has also created a family business that employs over six hundred persons, he is committed to creating jobs in the African American community, he along with his wife are the founders of the Black on Black Love Campaign, and he has bought and renovated the Regal Theater designed to bring entertainment to the Black community. Parren Mitchell, former congressman and major architect of the set-aside Program, Julianne Malveaux, a noted economist, Nkechi Taifa, a lawyer and one of the major advocates of reparations, and to make sure that we have some one who knows the Lord and is committed to his people, Rev. Jeremiah A. Wright, Jr. - two men; one of them a multi-millionaire, two women, and a minister.

Another idea that we've heard in the area of capital formation comes from Tony Brown and former congressman Walter Fauntroy. Their idea encourages larger African American organizations to quit spending three billion dollars annually at White hotels. If we collectively decided not to have conferences at White hotels for one year, we could save three billion dollars which could then be used to build four regional African American hotels with stores and theatres, and have additional monies for business loans, scholarships, and whatever else the committee would deem necessary. It is an excellent idea, but it requires the commitment of the organizations and its membership. I understand that for some organizations there is a structural problem that because of their size they've committed to hotels, signed contracts, and provided deposits four to six years in advance. Alterations will have to be made for those organizations, but I think the fundamental issue is attitude. Do we feel it is important to accumulate a base of capital to develop our own hotels so we no longer have to meet at their hotels? For others, the issue is middle class values such as sleeping in a suite at Master Hyatt, Hilton, and Marriott. I've heard some African Americans say they would not want to have a conference at a Black college temporarily while the Ramses, Nefertiti, and Garvey suites were being built.

The third idea we've heard from various people on this committee is that we have got to begin to secure more money from our athletes and entertainers. It has been said that we can finance our entire liberation struggle from some of the contributions from our athletes and entertainers. It is very difficult to develop this type of economy if our entertainers and athletes feel they need a 20-bedroom house with a bedroom shaped like boxing gloves. Some athletes and entertainers, for some reason, feel that they need a spouse outside of their race along with a lawyer, investor, and an agent of the dominant culture. We need to have a public disclosure of all our athletes and entertainers and who their lawyers, agents, and investors are and where they contribute their money. The obsession with sports in America has become unhealthy. The stadiums remind me of gladiator sports, where we play and the masters watch, while poor Black youth are unable to attend. Charles Barkley is correct, he's not a role model, he's a basketball player. Barkley encourages youth to respect and look up to the adults that care for them daily. We need to have Bill Cosby, Stevie Wonder, Oprah Winfrey, Craig Hodges, Dave Winfield, and Mel Blount form an African American committee to organize athletes and entertainers for liberation.

The same also applies to the church. If our largest institution has approximately 90 percent of its money in White banks and uses close to the same percentage of White general contractors to build their buildings that again reflects the dismal state of the Black economy. The congregation has to begin to demand for church leadership to deposit its money in Black banks.

The next area is Segmented Marketing. There are certain industries we should control if for no other reason than our dispro- portionate contribution. The four areas that I've heard mentioned from this committee are hair care, music, food, and clothing. We should attack them in that order because we have a greater chance of success in the former than the latter. For example, in the hair care industry there is the association of American Aids and Beauty Institute, a group of about 21 Black manufacturers that produce Black hair care products. They developed the African queen as a symbol of the association. Many of them do not have the advertising budget and the distribution channels of Revlon and Alberto Culver. These companies use Black bottles and Black advertising agencies and come across as if they are African American. African Americans presently control about 40 percent of this market. This market has been under siege over the past 10 years because White companies are very much aware of our desire to alter our "good hair."

The second industry where there is great potential is music. While some people are very critical of our "rappers" who have been progressive enough to begin to put on the table the fact that something is wrong if we are the major buyer in this industry and yet all the money seems to go to the recording companies, distributors, and retailers. Can you imagine the musical industry without Black talent? Well we may need to begin to imagine it because we need to seriously look at Black musicians only singing for Black recording labels and Black consumers only supporting Black recording labels. Of course White executives in the industry are very much aware of the divide and conquer strategy and so what they will continually do is to provide a large contract to a Michael Jackson, Diana Ross, Anita Baker, or M. C. Hammer. That can look very tempting to a new artist who initially is committed to the Black label, but the Black label initially can't compete. This is another industry that we need to control. The Greeks and Italians control the produce market, Asians control their food products and the cleaning industry, Jews controls the banking, legal, and mass media industries, and we need to control our music.

113

Rev. Sampson has mentioned that we also need to control our share of the food industry. We need to begin to have supermarkets in every major city and develop a product for international consumption, stocked with produce from Black farmers. There is no way we are going to build a strong economy if we are landless and can not feed ourselves. We are losing 500,000 acres of land annually. One third of our farmers have already gone out of business. This is an excellent opportunity to link the Black farmer with the Black consumer to connect the south with the north. We will build a beautiful soul food restaurant in the downtown area to break the enclave and economic detour. It will attract patrons from all ethnic groups. The last area that I think we have some potential in the clothing industry. When our people are killing each other over a pair of Nike tennis shoes and Starter Jackets that are made in South Korea for eight dollars and sold in the United States for a $150, then we need to begin to develop a manufacturing plant utilizing our southern, Caribbean, and African labor. Why should African medallions be made in Hong Kong versus Camden, Gary, East St. Louis, Tupelo, Jamaica, or Ghana?

The final proposal is reparations. Several people who are present here such as David Swinton, Benjamin Hooks, John Jacobs, John Conyers, Minister Farrakhan, members of the Hebrew Israelites, The Shrine of the Black Madonna, and numerous others have in one way or another endorsed reparations. It is pleasantly surprising that a diverse group agrees that a major infusion of capital maybe necessary to achieve parity. The income disparity between Africans and Europeans has remained inequitable for the past 20 or 30 years. At the present rate, it would take African Americans until the 23rd century to finally reach economic equality with the White community. The gap in wealth and business formation does not appear that it's going to close in the near future. Jesse Jackson has recommended the utilization of pension funds. John Jacobs has mentioned a Marshall Plan which is very similar to the concept of reparations. Reparations is now being considered before Congress. It becomes obvious that there's a widening income gap and greater housing segregation between the White and Black communities and between the Black haves and the Black have nots. Reparations may be the only way to create equality. How can we save the 609,000 Black men in prison and the 1 of 4 expected to enter? As much as

I'm an advocate of self-help and economic development, if we tripled Black businesses that would not substantially reduce the Black unemployment rate nor would it significantly increase Black wealth in America. I'm not naive enough to believe the Black conservatives' boot strap can eliminate the atrocities that have been placed on our people for the past 300 to 400 years. I'm also very much aware of the arguments that people present against reparations such as, it is naive for us to wait for this government out of its own benevolence to give us that kind of money. My response is the same as that of Frederick Douglass "Power concedes nothing without a struggle." At the same time I also feel that we need to develop our businesses areas while we have Congressman Conyers, Nkechi Taifa and others working in the area of reparations. Another argument that I've heard is that reparations for the Japanese were given to the immediate offspring of the people placed in the concentration camps. I don't think that it would be that difficult for us to document we did not come to America by Pan Am or TWA but by slave ships. Another response that I've heard is what would the enumeration be and would it be received by each individual African American or an organization. I propose along with the committee that reparations not be allocated to the individual but toward organizations that would coordinate college scholarships, business loans, land, and the other items mentioned at the Detroit conference in 1969.

The fundamental problem with business formation, product promotion and distribution, capital development and segmented marketing is lack of enforcement. A people who do not see themselves as a nation may not act in it's own best interest. Therefore, the only strategy that we can provide to address this issue is that we need to continue to educate our people on their identity, purpose, and direction. We need to change the values of our people from individualism, materialism and short-term gratification to collectivism, freedom, and long-term self-sufficiency. Until then, most individuals will not contribute to the National Black United Fund, alter conference plans, or support Black businesses. Most athletes, entertainers, and churches will not be supportive and accountable. There remains the option Mao implemented in China, where you kill all those who possess a non-liberation value system and you produce a new society with youth. Because of my relationship with the Lord, I can't endorse this option, so I will pray that the above solutions and others will be implemented. The reality is that America is not as concerned about cost-effectiveness and balancing the budget as it is about oppression, white supremacy, and the maintenance of power. It would be cheaper to eliminate paying a welfare recipient $240,000 and an inmate $800,000 ($20,000 x 40 years) by distributing reparations - unless oppression means more than economics.

In conclusion, I stated in the introduction six objectives for this book, let's review and implement them immediately.

1) We need to increase the number of businesses.

2) We need our talented "10th" starting businesses, rather than working for the government or Fortune 500 corporations.

3) We need a community that will encourage entrepreneurship and parents who promote a "good business" versus a "good job" to their children.

4) We need African American institutions to emphasize economic over political development.

5) We need to resist racism and advocate for governmental assistance.

6) We need business owners to provide quality products and service, who contribute back to the community, because they value liberation - not self- aggrandizement.

"Let's Get Busy" !

References

1) Introduction, Paul Pryde and Shelly Green. *Black Entrepreneurship in America.* (New Brunswick: Transaction Publishers, 1990), p. 26

CHAPTER ONE

1) David Swinton, *The Economic Status of African Americans:Permanent Poverty and Inequality, The State of Black America* (New York: National Urban League, 1991), pp.51-53.
2) Sydney Wilhelm, *Who Needs the Negro* (New York: Anchor Books, 1971), pp. 189-191.
3) William Tabb, *The Political Economy of the Black Ghetto* (New York: W.W. Norton, 1970), pp.21-34.
4) Swinton, op.cit. p.35
5) Gary Orfield and Carole Ashkinaze, *The Closing Door.* (Chicago: University of Chicago, 1991), p.46.
6) Swinton, op.cit. p.38.
7) Shelley Green and Paul Pryde, *Black Entrepreneurship in America* (New Brunswick: Transaction Publishers, 1990), pp. 12, 25.
8) Swinton. op.cit. p. 71.
9) ibid. p. 73.
10) Frank Fratoe, "Social Capital of Black Business Owners," *Review of Black Political Economy, Spring* 1988, Vol. 16, No. 4, p. 34.
11) Sam Fulwood III, "Against All Odds Business Start-ups Unstifled", *Emerge Magazine,* February 1991, p. 31.
12) Edward Pennick, "Land Ownership and Black Economic Development", *Black Scholar Magazine, January* 1990, Vol. 21, No. 1, p. 43.
13) Gary Orfield and Carole Ashkinaze, op.cit. pp. 53-56.
14) Eleanor Branch, "Competing For Contracts", *Black Enterprise.* February 1988, p. 205.

CHAPTER TWO

1) Julius Nyerere, *Ujamaa Essays on Socialism* (Dar es Salaam:Oxford University Press, 1968), p. 11.
2) Theodore Cross, *Black Power Imperative* (New York: Faulkner,1984), p. 56.

3) Nyerere, opcit p. 7.

4) Earl Ofari, *The Myth of Black Capitalism* (New York: Monthly Review Press, 1970), p. 15.

5) August Meir, *Negro Thought in America 1880-1915* (Ann Arbor: University of Michigan Press, 1966), pp. 125-126.

6) John Butler and Kenneth Wilson, *Entrepreneurial Enclaves in the African American Experience* (Washington: Neighborhood Policy Institute, 1990), pp. 27-28.

7) Manning Marable, *How Capitalism Underdeveloped Black America,* (Boston: South End Press, 1983), p. 144.

8) Butler and Wilson, opcit. pp. 17-20.

9) John Butler, *Entrepreneurship and Self-Help Among Black Americans* (Albany: Suny Press, 1991), pp. 171-172.

10) Ofari, opcit. pp. 39-43.

11) Butler, opcit. pp. 209-217.

12) Dorothy Lewis, "Forty Acres Fifty Dollars and a Mule with Interest", p. 16.

13) Ofari, opcit. pp. 103-106.

14) Cross, opcit. p. 76.

15) Ofari, opcit. p. 94.

CHAPTER THREE

1) Frank Fratoe, "A Sociological Analysis of Minority Businesses," *Review of Black Political Economy,* Fall 1986, Vol. 15, No. 2, p. 9.

2) Ivan Light, *Ethnic Enterprise in America* (Berkley: University of California Press, 1972), pp. 23-25.

3) Randall Brock, "The Future of Mom and Pop Businesses in the Black Community," *Crisis Magazine,* " May 1991, pp. 10-12.

4) Timothy Bates, "The Changing Nature of Minority Businesses," *The Review of Black Political Economy,* Fall 1989, Vol. 18, No. 2, pp. 26-32.

5) ibid. p. 33.

6) Molly Askin, "In the San Francisco Bay Area Blacks are Still Seeking an Economic Base and the Right to Prosper," *Crisis Magazine,* May 1991, p. 28.

CHAPTER FOUR

1) Holly Sklar, ed. *Trilateralism* (Boston: South End Press, 1981), p. 3.

2) Robert Reich, *The Work of Nations* (New York: Knopf, 1991), p. 119.

3) ibid. p. 115.

4) ibid. pp. 120-123.

5) ibid. pp. 126-127.

6) ABC, "Nightline," May 20, 1991, Ted Koppel host.

7) Reich, opcit. pp. 128-129.

8) ibid. p. 146-147.

CHAPTER FIVE

1) David Swinton, *The Economic Status of African Americans: Permanent Poverty and Inequality, The State of Black America 1991* (New York: National Urban League, 1991), pp. 29, 72.

2) National Business Incubation Association. Industry Fact Sheet Athens, Ohio, 1991.

3) George Subira, Black Folks Guide to Business Success (Newark: Very Serious Business, 1986), pp. 74-75.

4) Joseph Pierce, *Negro Business and Business Education.* (New York: Harper & Row 1947) p. 52.

5) Paul Pryde and Shelley Green, *Black Entrepreneurship in America* (New Brunswick: Transaction Publishers, 1990), p. 38.

6) Timothy Bates, "The Changing Nature of Minority Businesses: A Comparative Analysis of Asian, Non-Minority and Black-Owned Business," *Review of Black Political Economy,* Fall 1989, Vol. 18, No. 2, p. 33.

CHAPTER SIX

1) Nancy Ryan, "Marketing to Black Consumers," *Chicago Tribune,* June 9, 1991, section 7, p. 6.
Tony Brown's Speech, May 20, 1990, Freedom Fund Dinner, Jackson, Tennessee.

2) David Swinton, *The Economic Status of African Americans: Permanent Poverty and Inequality The State of Black America 1991* (New York: National Urban League, 1991), pp. 28-39, 67.
Minority Business Report. WGN Television Show, June 15, 1990.

3) Ohio State Black Economic Conference May 1990. Personal Finance Workshop, Tape # 39.

4) Joel Kotkin and Yoriko Kishimoto, The Third Century (New York: Crown Publishers, 1988), p. 112.

5) Scott Witt, How Self Made Millionaires Build Their Fortunes (West Nyach: Parker Publishing, 1979), p. 15, 17.

6) George Subira, *Black Folks Guide to Making Big Money in America* (Newark: Very Serious Business, 1980), p. 50.

7) Derek Dingle, "An Agenda For the Black Middle Class," *Black Enterprise,* November 1989, p. 60.

8) Shelley Green and Paul Pryde, Black Entrepreneurship in America (New Brunswick: Transaction Publishers, 1990), p. 12.

9) William Bradford and Timothy Bates, *Financing Black Economic Development* (New York: Academic Press, 1979), pp. 34, 61.

David Swinton, "The Economic Status of African Americans: 'Permanent' Poverty and Inequality," *The State of Black America* 1991 (New York: National Urban League 1991) p. 38.

10) Venita Van Caspel, *The Power of Money Dynamics* (Reston: Reston Publishing, 1983), pp. 29-30.

11) Julianne Malveaux, Plenary Speech at Ohio State University, Black Economics Conference, May 1991.

12) George Subira, *Getting Black Folks to Sell* (Newark: Very Serious Business, 1988), p. 28.

CHAPTER SEVEN

1) Robert Woodson, *Race and Economic Opportunity* (Washington: National Center for Neighborhood Enterprise, 1989), p. 26.

2) George Subira, B*lack Folks' Guide to Business Success* (Newark: Very Serious Business Enterprises, 1986), pp. 95-99.

3) U.S. Small Business Administration. Focus on the Facts, No. 8 of a Series.

4) Rick Reiff, "Hatching Small Companies," *Your Company Magazine,* Winter 1991, pp. 36-39. National Business Incubation Association, Athens, Ohio, Industry Fact Sheet. 1991.

5) Wiley Woodard, "Beyond Fast Food," *Black Enterprise,* September 1990, pp. 47-58, 73-75.

6) Eleanor Branch, "Competing for Contracts," *Black Enterprise.* February 1988, pp. 204-207.

7) B. Wright. O'Connor, "What's Next For The SBA," *Black Enterprise,* June 1989, p. 138.

8) Alex Pansett, "Paving The Path To 8 (A) Contracts," *Black Enterprise,* February 1989, p. 160.

Glossary

Accounts payable - an unpaid invoice.

Accounts receivable - an accounting term illustrating the customer owes a company.

Accrued - earned interest reinvested in the present account.

Amortization - an accounting schedule of a liability showing its reduction with each payment.

Annuity - investment instrument from an insurance company reinvesting guaranteed interest and deferred taxation.

Asset - collateral.

Balance sheet - an accounting term comparing assets to accounts payable and net worth.

Blue chip - stocks from a nationally recognized company with a history of paying dividends.

Bonds - a promissory note from a public or private corporation paying interest.

Book value - the value of a stock by dividing the net worth of a company by the number of outstanding stocks.

Break-even - the point where sales is equivalent to cost.

Capital - monies available for investment.

Capital gain - the profit from the sale of an asset.

Cash flow - an analysis of available cash and current expenses.

Collateral - assets pledged by a borrower to secure a loan.

Common stock - the purchase of shares in a company creating ownership.

Cost of goods sold - the dollar value of inventory consumed to generate sales.

Credit - an accounting term indicating an addition to accounts payable and net worth or deletion of accounts payable and net worth.

Debit - an accounting term indicating an addition to an asset or expense account.

Demand - the consumer's desire for a product.

Depreciation - the adjustment of an asset due to usage.

Diversification - the spreading of assets among various investment alternatives.

Dividend - the payment by a company to its shareholders.

Elasticity - the ratio of demand to price changes.

Entrepreneur - a person who owns a business.

Equity - the dollar value held by share holders and also the value after all payables were made.

Face value - the amount stated on the bond which is paid off at maturity.

Gross - profit after cost of goods sold.

Gross national product - the total sales of a country's business.

Intangible - Invisible assets such as goodwill.

Interest - earned income from an investment.

Inventory - merchandise.

Leverage - the use of collateral to secure loans for the purpose   of investments at higher rates of return.

Liability - an outstanding obligation.

Limited partnership - a legal investment arrangement where a person's liability is equivalent to their investment.

Liquid - assets that are in cash form or could be in a very short term period.

Load - the charge against the investor by the brokerage firm.

Market value - the value of a stock as determined by the demand of customers purchasing on the stock exchange.

Maturity - an asset that was invested over a time period that is now expiring.

Monopoly - an industry dominated by a few companies.

Multiplier - the effect of the same dollar being received by different businesses in a short period of time within a defined geographical or cultural area.

Mutual funds - the purchase of stock from an investment company which will invest in a collection of companies.

Net - profit after all expenses.

Net worth - the value of an entity after liabilities.

Overhead - fixed expenses primarily rent and utilities.

Portfolio - the total picture of a person's assets.

Preferred stock - the purchase of stock with rights to dividends before common shareholders.

Prime rate - the lowest interest available to customers determined by the Federal Reserve Board.

Reconciliation - the adjustment of an account, normally between a bank and a customer.

Royalty - percentage of revenue for literary or artistic contribution.

Split - the division of outstanding shares of a corporation creating more shares at less value for present holders.

Supply - the company's ability to provide the product.

Tangible - concrete visible assets.

Trust - a legal document similar to a will explaining the distribution of assets at death.

Vested - a position achieved by an employee based on seniority in a profit sharing or pension plan.

Yield - ratio of return, profit from an investment.